D1614142

CORVETTE
CHRONICLE

**BY JAMES FLAMMANG AND
THE AUTO EDITORS OF CONSUMER GUIDE®**

Publications
International, Ltd.

Copyright © 1993 Publications International, Ltd. All rights reserved. This book may not be reproduced or quoted in whole or in part by mimeograph or any other printed or electronic means, or for presentation on radio, television, videotape, or film without written permission from:

Louis Weber, C.E.O.
Publications International, Ltd.
7373 North Cicero Avenue
Lincolnwood, Illinois 60646

Permission is never granted for commercial purposes.

Manufactured in USA.

8 7 6 5 4 3 2 1

ISBN: 0-7853-0068-6

CREDITS:

Owners
Special thanks to the owners of the cars featured in this book for their enthusiastic cooperation. They are listed below along with the page number(s) on which their cars appear:

Dorothy Clemmer: 12 **Dr. Ernie Hendry:** 12, 13 **Dave Stefun:** 19, 20, 21 **David Ferguson:** 20, 21 **Jeff Dranson:** 24, 25 **Edward S. Kuziel:** 25 **Noel Blanc:** 28 **Robert & Diane Adams:** 29, 39 **Ed Dwyer:** 30 **Thomas J. Witt:** 30 **Pete Bogard:** 31 **Chip Werstein:** 43 **Thomas Crockatt:** 44, 45 **Fred Grasseschi:** 47 **Richard Carpenter:** 48 **Don Maich:** 49 **Gary Girt:** 52, 53 **Crystal Endicott:** 52 **Chuck Swafford:** 53 **John Rikert:** 53 **Phillip & Sandy Lopiccold:** 58 **William Bauce:** 58 **K.D. James:** 59 **David Anderson:** 59 **Tom Schay:** 60 **Bruce Jacobs:** 61 **Robert Paterson:** 62, 63 **Edward Mueller:** 63 **Howard L. Baker:** 66, 67 **Carlos & Sherry Vivas:** 67 **Jim Leinart:** 71 **Robert Kleckauskas:** 72 **Scott Mase:** 73 **John Baritel:** 75 **Gary Jimenez:** 76 **Richard Carpenter:** 77 **Eric Coleman:** 77 **Edward Klujian:** 78, 80 **Cynthia Rekemeyer:** 79 **Marty & Jacque Wetzgar:** 80 **Roger Judski:** 80 **Bill Kitchum:** 81 **Alan R. Oakley:** 81 **Allan Cummins:** 82 **Gary Mills:** 83 **"T" & Ed DeCamp:** 87 **Ben Oliver:** 88 **Roger Jodski:** 89 **Mike Vietro:** 92 **Frank Capolipo:** 93 **Dan & Joyce Lyons:** 95 **Charles A. Vance:** 97 **Don Jeri:** 101 **Kirk Alexander:** 103 **Mark Alter:** 112, 113 **Roseanne Winney:** 120, 121 **Peter Zannis:** 124 **California Custom Coach:** 129 **Gordon & Dorothy Clemmer:** 130, 131 **Corvette Mike:** 136, 142, 184 **Edward E. Oritz:** 147 **John M. Endres:** 158 **A.R. Bartz:** 168.

Photo Acknowledgments
The editors would like to thank the following people and organizations for supplying the photography that made this book possible. They are listed below, along with the page number(s) of their photos:

Mitch Frumkin—185-186, 188-189; **Dan Gingerelli**—102, 105, 108-110; **Greenwood Automotive**—191; **Sam Griffith**—31, 72, 166-167, 178, 182-183, 187; **Jerry Heasley**—59, 100, 104-105; **S. Scott Hutchinson**—30; **Bud Juneau**—19, 20, 49, 62-63, 72, 158, 168; **Milton Gene Kieft**—52-53, 66-67; **Bill Kilborn**—12, 13, 46, 77, 80, 89; **Bill Locke**—99; **Dan Lyons**—47, 79, 95; **Vince Manocchi**—12, 15, 20, 28, 39, 43-45, 48, 58, 60-61, 67, 75, 77, 80, 82, 88, 93, 97, 112, 120-121, 130-131, 136, 142, 147, 184; **Doug Mitchel**—30, 58, 71, 78, 80-81, 83, 92, 101, 135; **Mike Mueller**—25; **Owens-Corning**—89; **D. Randy Riggs**—103, 186, 188-189; **Shinoda-Williams Designs, Inc.**—179; **Rick Voegelin, High Performance Communications**—189; **Nicky Wright**—52, 59, 76, 87, 103.

Very Special Thanks to: Kari St. Antoine & Mark Broderick, Chevrolet Public Relations; Chuck Jordan, Former Vice President GM Design; Floyd Joliet, GM Design Staff; Ginny & Burt Greenwood, Greenwood Automotive, Sanford Florida; Brian Broadbent, Mike Vietro, Corvette Mike, Orange California; Sue Burkett, Owens-Corning Public Relations; Ron McQueeney, Indianapolis Motor Speedway Corp.; Lisa Shinoda, Shinoda-Williams Design, Inc., Livonia, Michigan.

C O N T

E N T S

FOREWORD

Who could have guessed, when General Motors displayed its hastily-created little roadster at the 1953 Motorama, that a legend was in the making? Sure, the bright white, open-topped two-seater was cute and capable of inspiring a host of romantic fantasies. And, yes, it drew eager attention. But so did the imported sports cars that had been staging a modest, yet escalating invasion of U.S. shores.

After all, this wasn't the breed of automobile that the newly-prosperous, red-blooded Americans craved. American motorists wanted big cars, flashy cars, with brawny V-8 engines coupled to automatic transmissions.

Or did they? GM soon would find out when it elected to transform its appealing little show car into a production model.

Up to that time, the handful of postwar American two-seaters were the work of independent automakers and small entrepreneurs, not giants like GM. Nash had its Nash-Healey, Kaiser-Frazer its Kaiser-Darrin. Even the Crosley organization had issued a sporty Hot Shot. Briggs Cunningham was stuffing big Chrysler "hemi" V-8s into Italian-styled GT bodies, and Earl "Mad Man" Muntz had turned the Kurtis Sport into his own Muntz Jet.

But none of these vehicles lasted more than a couple of years. In fact, sports cars of every stripe took only 0.3 percent of the burgeoning U.S. market in 1953.

The American fascination with speed and sport dated back to such rakish machines as the 1911-15 Mercer Raceabout and the Stutz Bearcat. Less-affluent speed demons turned to hot rodding, driving stripped-down Fords with souped-up flat-head V-8s. The lure of speed and a combination of other events led to the introduction of the Corvette. There was a growing need for a truly American sports car.

Servicemen returning from Europe set this trend into motion when many of them brought back sports cars. Most often, it was the quaintly old-fashioned, but exciting, British-built MG TC. Crude and rough riding, but delightfully charming, these were fragile-looking roadsters, with bucket seats and floor shifts—an archaic mechanism that had departed from most U.S. autos before the war. The sporty two-seaters also handled with agility, a world apart from the boatlike behemoths with which most Americans were enthralled.

By 1950, the TC gave way to a more modern MG TD, and to the debut of the stunning Jaguar XK-120 roadster. Then came the equally British Austin-Healey, and the Triumph TRs. Other sports cars trickled in from Italy: Alfa Romeo, Fiat, Maserati. Soon, the Germans entered the fray, led by the gullwing Mercedes-Benz 300SL.

By then, the Sports Car Club of America had been formed and rallies begun. Sports-car fans roamed the nation's byways in their mostly-foreign machines, waving greetings as they crossed paths.

General Motors, meanwhile, had solidified its role as auto-industry leader. First came the "Futuramic" 1948 Olds and tail-finned Cadillac, followed by the overhead-valve V-8 and the "hardtop convertible" body.

Dominating the field, GM was actually in the best position to turn to a low-volume sports car. However, it came down to some strong personalities at the corporation—men able to foresee the prospects for a sporty roadster—that pushed for the Corvette's introduction.

Their names are no less legendary than the car itself. Harley Earl, dubbed the "father" of Detroit styling, had largely developed the "dream car" concept with his '38 Buick Y-Job—a car which gave GM the inspiration for its Motorama shows of 1949-61. These shows gave customers a sneak peek at future styling. Specifically, the 1953 Motorama and its star, the Corvette, were the zenith of Earl's career.

Another key player in the Corvette's genesis, and a man who would soon become chief Corvette engineer, was Zora Arkus-Duntov. He believed there was indeed a market for a domestic sports car—provided it was built to American tastes, for American roads.

Other legendary names would come later: Bill Mitchell, Earl's successor as head of GM styling . . . Ed Cole, whose foremost legacy was the small-block V-8 that's powered most 'Vettes . . . David McLellan, carrying Corvette into the modern era . . . Jerry Palmer, who led styling of the sixth (current) generation . . . Chuck Jordan, recently retired as head of GM Design.

What helped it all come together was glass-reinforced plastic (GRP). Developed during the war, GRP was used to create the Glasspar roadster (sold in kit form or assembled) and the Woodill Wildfire, hailed as the first "production" fiberglass sports car. Their intriguing, if numerically limited, success inspired Harley Earl, who borrowed the idea for the Corvette.

Customers didn't exactly arrive in droves. Not at first, anyway. Corvette, in fact, came close to extinction more than once over the years; but it survived, and drew a growing legion of avid fans. A full 39 years and six styling generations later, on July 2, 1992, the millionth Corvette rolled off the line. And now that the car's 40th birthday has been marked by a special anniversary edition for '93, we await the forthcoming seventh generation.

What's kept it going? In a word, tradition. Far more than most automobiles, Corvette has stuck close to its origins. By the time the first Chevy V-8 appeared, the die had been cast. Although the timeless vehicle billed as "America's only *true* sports car" has evolved steadily over the years, its basic structure has not been changed—or compromised—since 1955.

Our thanks go to the owners of the Corvettes pictured so vividly in these pages. We congratulate the Chevrolet Motor Division and the GM Design Staff on the 40th anniversary of the legendary Corvette (1953-93).

—The Auto Editors of CONSUMER GUIDE®

1953

Dwight D. Eisenhower was sworn in as 34th president of the U.S., with Richard M. Nixon as vice-president. After more than three years of conflict, the Korean War ended on July 27, 1953.

Julius and Ethel Rosenberg died in the electric chair in June, convicted of selling U.S. secrets to the Soviets.

In Chicago, Hugh Hefner produced the first issue of *Playboy* magazine.

GM head Charles Wilson declared that "for many years I thought what was good for our country was good for General Motors, and vice-versa." Richard and Mac McDonald selected an odd shape for their hamburger shop in San Bernardino, California: a pair of golden arches.

•EX-122 prototype appears at GM Motorama, starting in New York in January 1953

•First Corvette rolls off the line on June 30; makes press debut in September

•Each fiberglass-bodied two-seater is Polo White, with red/white interior

•Corvette power comes from a Blue Flame six-cylinder engine, hopped up to 150 bhp, with Powerglide automatic

•300 Corvettes built at Flint, Michigan, in 1953, before production moves to St. Louis at end of year

•Overall, Chevrolet tops Ford production by 100,000

▲ GM's Motorama Corvette, seen at New York's Waldorf Astoria Hotel, was carried over virtually line-for-line to the production Corvette. Actual cars deleted hydraulic-opening doors and hood, fan shroud, and other details.

▼ Sleek, low lines of the Motorama show car are particularly striking when seen alongside a 1953 Chevrolet Bel Air sedan. Engine revisions were needed to clear the Corvette's low hood.

▲ The Corvette's fiberglass body was made of 46 pieces, supplied by the Molded Fiber Glass Company of Ashtabula, Ohio, and then turned into larger assemblies. However, in the early cars the bodies lagged in fit and finish.

▲ Cut-away view details the placement of the Blue Flame Six to the rear of the front axle. The chassis was modified Chevrolet, with center of gravity only 18 inches above ground. Steering was quickened to a 16:1 ratio.

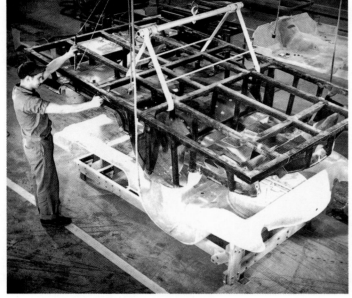

▲ During body assembly, a drill jig was lowered over the Corvette's reinforced plastic underbody to serve as a guide for hole locations. Rivets enhanced the security of the bond.

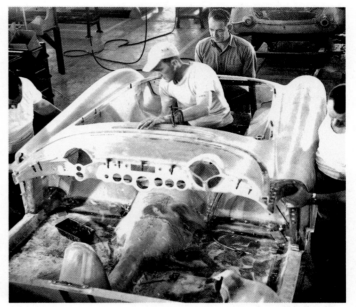

▲ Workers assemble the front top section to the underbody—the Corvette's basic structure—which has been fitted with the instrument panel and the lower portion of the seatback.

▲ Many call Harley J. Earl, founder of GM Art & Colour and stylist of the '27 LaSalle, the "father" of Corvette.

▲ Chevrolet's St. Louis plant housed the world's only plastic body assembly line. Soon after production moved from Flint in late December 1953, one unit was being created every 10 minutes—a startling pace for a then new technology.

▲ On June 30, 1953, the first three of 300 white Corvettes rolled off the line. Each was meant for VIPs.

▲ Zora Arkus-Duntov, later to be head engineer, called the first Corvette "the most beautiful car [he] had ever seen."

▶ A worker demonstrates inherent lightness of the fiberglass body shell. Chevrolet boasted that it was "very stable . . . of light weight, able to stand up to abuse [and] will not rust [or] crumble in a collision."

▲ First-generation Corvettes featured a vertical-toothed grille and stone guards. All '53s had a Delco signal-seeking radio, hot-water heating, and engine revolution counter.

▼ Tricks used to tweak 150 bhp out of the Blue Flame Special six-cylinder engine included triple sidedraft carbs and 8.0:1 compression. Two-speed Powerglide was the only transmission available.

▲ Though attractive and symmetrical, the twin-pod dashboard had gauges spread across its width. This made readings difficult, particularly the center-mounted 5000-rpm tachometer.

▼▲ Smooth bodysides extended into a pair of jet-pod tail-lights, capped by mini fins. Short dual-exhaust extensions sat inboard of rear fenders. Bumpers offered minimal protection. Clip-in side curtains, as in British roadsters, didn't please all Americans. Neither did the plastic-covered rear license housing. Purists scoffed, but testers praised the car's handling.

▲ Interiors came only in Sportsman Red, with white lower dashboard surround and steering wheel (one inch smaller in diameter than other Chevrolets). Bucket seats and a floor-mounted gearshift lever weren't everyday sights in American vehicles of 1953. The soft folding top fit beneath a flush-fit cover. Because doors held no handles or pushbuttons, the driver had to reach inside to gain entry.

▲ Chevy's 235.5-cid six developed 150 horsepower at 4500 rpm under Corvette hoods, thanks to triple Carter "YH" carburetors and a high-lift, long-duration camshaft with solid lifters. Also, dual valve springs helped handle the higher engine speed. Dual exhausts improved breathing and reverberated in a pleasing tone.

▲ Each carburetor fed two cylinders. Motorama cars had an automatic choke, but production versions were manual. Early 'Vettes had a twin-handle hood latch.

Earl Warren was confirmed as Chief Justice of the Supreme Court in March. Two months later, in a unanimous decision, the Court ruled that school segregation was unequal.

In an April speech, President Eisenhower put forth the "domino theory," claiming that Asian nations could fall one after the other to Communist forces. Millions watched the Army-McCarthy hearings, as Senator Joseph McCarthy and counsel Roy Cohn countered charges of misconduct during their four-year anti-Red crusade.

Dr. Jonas Salk's polio vaccine was approved, soon to ease this scourge that had plagued young lives. Seven out of 10 American families now owned cars.

Father Knows Best premiered as a TV series, and actor Ronald Reagan was hired to host TV's *General Electric Theater.*

• Second-year Corvettes come in a choice of four colors

• Corvette sales lag behind expectations, though 3640 find customers

• Various running changes appear during the year

• Two Corvette-based "dream cars" appear: a Corvair fastback and Nomad wagon

• Ford's production beats Chevrolet by 22,381—new Ford V-8 engine gets credit

• GM produces its 50-millionth car in November

▲ At the St. Louis plant a fiberglass body is dropped onto the chassis. While the Motorama show car body was ²/₁₀-inch thick, the production body was but ¹/₁₀-inch thick.

▲ This factory shot emphasized just how low the '54 Corvette really was. Though list-priced at $3523, the advertised base figure dipped as low as $2774. Powerglide became a $178 "mandatory" option, however, and heater and accessories added to the base price.

Agile performance

Sensational styling

Luxurious comfort

▲ The sales brochure promised a mix of performance, style and comfort, aimed at "sports-loving, fun-loving people" who were "young at heart."

1954 Selected Colors

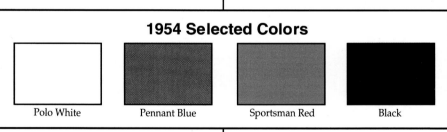

Polo White   Pennant Blue   Sportsman Red   Black

▲ The folding top, now tan instead of black, hid beneath a hinged lid. Side curtains slipped into a bag. To keep the license recess dry, desiccant bags were included. During the model run, longer exhaust tips were installed to deflect noxious gases away from the body.

◄ In addition to the original Polo White, which accounted for four-fifths of production, this year's two-seater came in Pennant Blue and Sportsman Red. A few were black. Changes included a single-handle hood latch, and better-protected gas and brake lines. The choke moved left of the steering column.

▲ As part of an April 27, 1954, dealer driveaway and publicity stunt, 41 new Corvettes streamed through the S-curve on Chicago's Lake Shore Drive. All had dealer plates and featured mesh-covered headlights and jet-pod taillights.

▲ Another dealer driveaway, like this publicity parade on the Los Angeles Harbor Freeway, helped drum up excitement. Even so, some Corvettes remained unsold at year's end. Sports-car purists tended to sneer at Chevy's pretty roadster.

◀ Whether at the race tracks or on public roads, Chevrolet liked to publicize its fiberglass sportster. The tri-carb six-cylinder engine got a new camshaft and 5 more horsepower at mid-year. A Corvette could hit 60 mph in 11 seconds.

▼ A Corvette with removable hardtop appeared at the 1954 Motorama. A Harley J. Earl idea, it turned the roadster into a thin-pillar coupe, complementing the wraparound windshield.

▲ Note the pillar louvers and large license plate recess at the rear of the dramatic Corvair fastback (*foreground*).

▲ Never considered for production, the Corvette-based Nomad was strictly a show wagon, set up for six passengers.

▲ Behind a stock model sit a trio of Corvette-based show cars that toured the 1954 Motorama circuit: a roadster with lift-off hardtop and roll-up windows, Corvair fastback coupe, and Nomad wagon. No fastback was to appear until the Sting Ray of 1963, and the Corvair name would go to Chevy's rear-engine compact.

▲ The Motorama show car with lift-off roof was intended for production, but delayed two years. Late in the 1954 run, soft-top irons were redesigned so they slipped between the body and seatback.

▲ Despite its Corvette styling and engine, the Nomad show car was built on a standard 1953 wagon chassis. When Nomad emerged for 1955-57 as a full-size Chevy, it had similar upper body lines but not the Corvette look below.

1955

Military advisers were sent to Vietnam in February. The U.S. Senate voted 84-0 to continue investigating Communist activities by government workers. The Montgomery, Alabama, bus boycott began in December, setting the stage for civil rights protests into the 1960s.

Colonel Harlan Sanders started his Kentucky Fried Chicken franchises, and "Ann Landers" wrote her first advice column. Disneyland opened in July, and the hourly minimum wage rose from 75 cents to one dollar.

Brooding teen idol James Dean was killed in September at the wheel of his Porsche. Bill Haley's ditty, *Rock Around the Clock*, hit No. 1 on the music charts after it was featured in the movie *The Blackboard Jungle*.

• Top news: All Chevrolets may be ordered with small-block 265-cid V-8 engine

• Corvette V-8 develops 195 bhp; manual gearbox available late in year

• Despite V-8 and improved workmanship, production of little-changed Corvette sinks to 674 units

• Two-seat Ford Thunderbird bows, sells 16,155 copies; its success prompts Chevy to hang onto Corvette

• American production sets new record at 7,950,377 cars and 1,249,576 trucks

• LaSalle II show car wears Corvette-like body coves

▲ Had Chevrolet undertaken a proposed facelift, the '55 Corvette might have looked like this clay model, shot on March 4, 1954. Note the eggcrate grille mesh, similar to that used in full-size Chevrolets. Styling touches included a side chrome spear under fake vents, hood scoop, and exhaust tips that were moved outward.

▲ Lack of funds and weak sales meant the '55 Corvette would change little—except for a new V-8 engine. Here, a 'Vette runs the Pure Oil Trials at Daytona Beach. A production V-8 could hit 60 mph in 8.5 seconds and top off near 120 mph.

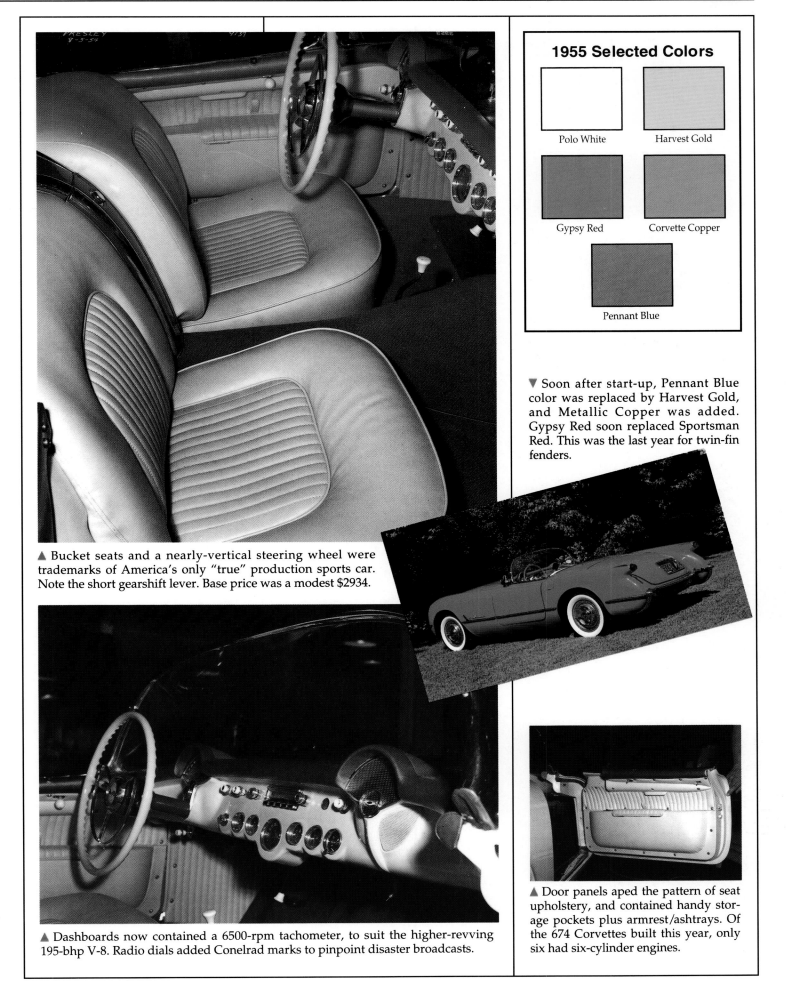

1955 Selected Colors

Polo White

Harvest Gold

Gypsy Red

Corvette Copper

Pennant Blue

▼ Soon after start-up, Pennant Blue color was replaced by Harvest Gold, and Metallic Copper was added. Gypsy Red soon replaced Sportsman Red. This was the last year for twin-fin fenders.

▲ Bucket seats and a nearly-vertical steering wheel were trademarks of America's only "true" production sports car. Note the short gearshift lever. Base price was a modest $2934.

▲ Dashboards now contained a 6500-rpm tachometer, to suit the higher-revving 195-bhp V-8. Radio dials added Conelrad marks to pinpoint disaster broadcasts.

▲ Door panels aped the pattern of seat upholstery, and contained handy storage pockets plus armrest/ashtrays. Of the 674 Corvettes built this year, only six had six-cylinder engines.

Real driving comfort . . . the Corvette way!

SECURITY AND LUXURY for driver and passenger are the keynotes of the snug Corvette cockpit. Individual bucket seats have form-fitting foam rubber cushions. The floor is covered in soft carpeting, backed by sponge rubber. Large pockets and ash trays in doors also serve as arm rests. Beautifully balanced instrument panel includes key-turn starter, electric clock, tachometer, hooded radio speaker.

POTENT "BLUE-FLAME" 6 engine, with three side-draft carburetors, 8 to 1 compression ratio, and overhead valves, puts a flashing 155 horsepower under the throttle. It has a dual exhaust system, efficient cooling and lubrication, and a shielded electrical system . . . plus Chevrolet's traditional six-cylinder economy of operation and maintenance.

A cyclone of power
with the new 195-h.p. V8 engine

A breath-stopping surge of power that surpasses anything you have ever imagined—that's the story of the Corvette's new 195-h.p. V8 engine. Here is a "dream" power-plant . . . ultra-compact, free-breathing, super-efficient, the most modern valve-in-head V8 engine in the world . . . and it can be serviced by any Chevrolet dealer. Dual exhausts, a four-barrel carburetor, 8 to 1 compression ratio, and a high-lift camshaft squeeze latent energy out of every drop of gasoline . . . and careful counter-balancing of the entire engine *after assembly* keeps it smooth as a jet of steam.

Geared-to-the-road stability

The Corvette is a sports car . . . not a scaled-down convertible. At any speed it offers a sense of security, an inherent balance that is astonishing. Low-slung, with a center of gravity only 18 inches above the pavement, its outrigger rear springs and broad-based front tread let it cling to the road like a cat. The steering gear has 16 to 1 ratio for instant response. Its big 11-inch brakes have bonded linings and a grip that would stop a truck. Everything is designed to give the absolute, precise command that only the driver of a true sports car can know.

▲ Chevrolet promoted the '55 model as having "Real *driving* comfort," a far cry from the truth when Ford's new T-Bird had roll-up windows and a hardtop. Nonetheless the '55 Corvettes had smoother bodies of slightly thinner section. Fit and finish were tighter and neater.

▶ Bucket seats were upholstered in vinyl, with complementary-colored interior accents. An automatic choke was now installed, along with 12-volt electricals for the V-8. Electric wipers replaced the vacuum unit, and a foot-operated windshield washer returned.

▲ Folding tops again hid within a flush-fitting lid. Chevrolet promoted luggage space as "generous," with the spare tire located under the floor of the trunk.

▲ Final first-generation 'Vettes kept covered headlights and tiny, body-mounted bumpers, but handled and performed better than ever.

▼ Big "V" in fender script proclaimed V-8 sizzle. The milestone small-block with independent rocker arms was Chevy's second V-8; the first came in 1917.

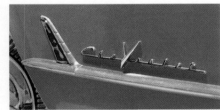

◄ Leading off a long parade of hot, V-8 Corvettes was the legendary 265-cid Turbo-Fire. With a four-barrel carb, it boasted 195 bhp at 5000 rpm, yet weighed 30-40 pounds less than the six.

ENGINE SPECS
1955

Type:	ovh I-6	ovh V-8
Bore X stroke (in.):	3.56 X 3.95	3.75 X 3.00
Displacement (ci):	235.5	265
Compression ratio:	8.0:1	8.0:1
Horsepower @ rpm (bhp):	155 @ 4200	195 @ 5000
Torque @ rpm (lbs/feet):	223 @ 2400	260 @ 3000
Fuel Delivery:	3 Carter sidedraft	1 X 4-bbl.
Transmission:	Powerglide	3-speed manual, optional Powerglide

DIMENSIONS

Wheelbase (in.):	102.0
Overall length (in.):	167.0
Overall height (in.):	52.2
Overall width (in.):	72.2
Track front/rear (in.):	56.7/58.8
Curb weight (lbs):	2910

Soviet Premier Nikita Khrushchev warned the U.S. that "... history is on our side. We will bury you." The Suez Crisis erupted after Egypt seized the Suez Canal. In November, Soviet tanks rolled into Hungary to crush a rebel uprising.

After a boycott in Montgomery, Alabama, the Supreme Court ruled bus segregation unconstitutional.

The Highway Act authorized a 41,000-mile Interstate Highway Network, with the federal government to pay 90 percent of costs. The Eisenhower-Nixon ticket won a second term.

Elvis Presley appeared on the *Ed Sullivan Show* in September, drawing a record 54 million viewers. This year's best-seller list included Grace Metalious's steamy *Peyton Place*. William Whyte chronicled American conformity in *The Organization Man.*

• Restyled second-generation Corvette offers choice of three V-8 engines: 210 to 240 bhp

• Top engine delivers 0-60 acceleration in 7.5 seconds

• New concave bodyside coves permit two-toning

• Roll-up windows replace the early side curtains, and lift-off hardtop is optional

• Three Corvettes finish the grueling Sebring road race

• Corvette production rises to 3467; Chevrolet builds 1.56 million cars, to Ford's 1.4 million

▲ Clay mockup from February 1, 1955, looks close to final '56 design, including the new bodyside coves.

▲ Another clay mockup from February 1955 features indents behind both the front and rear wheels.

▲ Final design for '56 was virtually locked in by the time of this full-size clay mockup, dated May 16, 1955.

▲ Note lack of chrome trim around the bodyside coves on this May 1955 full-size mockup, with hardtop in place.

▲ Side exhausts in the rear fenders of this February 1955 clay didn't make production, nor did certain body trim.

▲ Front indent on this clay is shorter than found used on the actual '56 Corvette, but the overall look was set.

▲ Headlights moved to a conventional position, and "frenched" taillights replaced the jet-pod design.

▲ Final styling was squarer up front, rounder in rear. Buyers appreciated the optional hardtop and roll-up windows.

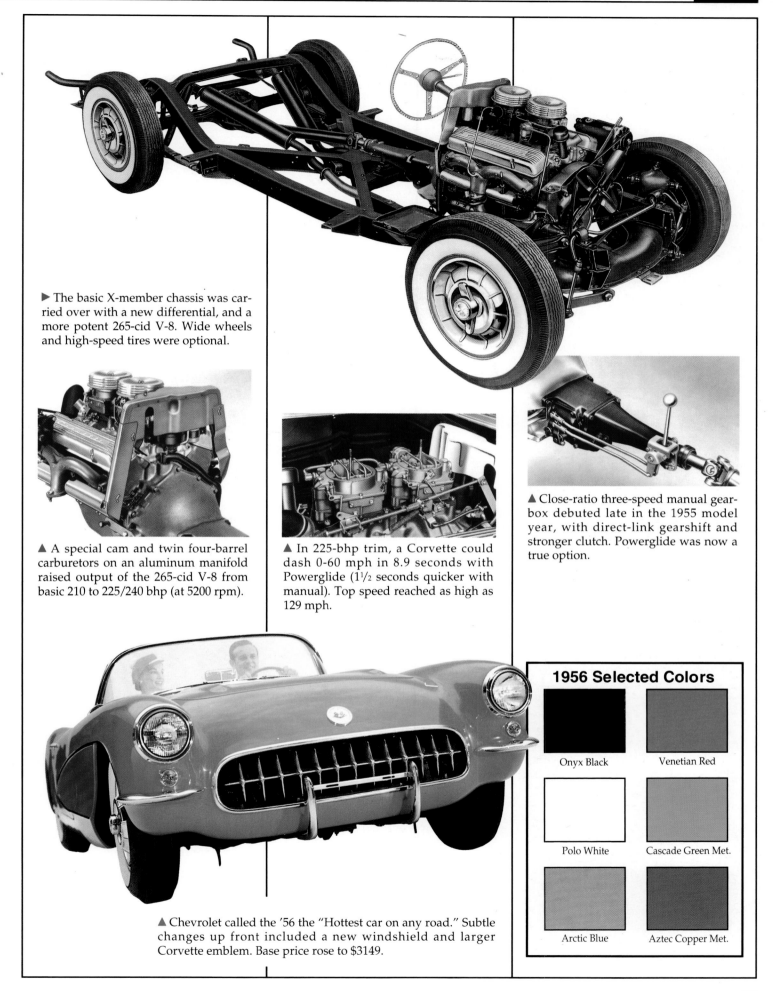

▶ The basic X-member chassis was carried over with a new differential, and a more potent 265-cid V-8. Wide wheels and high-speed tires were optional.

▲ A special cam and twin four-barrel carburetors on an aluminum manifold raised output of the 265-cid V-8 from basic 210 to 225/240 bhp (at 5200 rpm).

▲ In 225-bhp trim, a Corvette could dash 0-60 mph in 8.9 seconds with Powerglide (1½ seconds quicker with manual). Top speed reached as high as 129 mph.

▲ Close-ratio three-speed manual gearbox debuted late in the 1955 model year, with direct-link gearshift and stronger clutch. Powerglide was now a true option.

▲ Chevrolet called the '56 the "Hottest car on any road." Subtle changes up front included a new windshield and larger Corvette emblem. Base price rose to $3149.

1956 Selected Colors

Onyx Black

Venetian Red

Polo White

Cascade Green Met.

Arctic Blue

Aztec Copper Met.

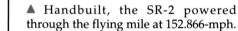

A NEW CORVETTE
BY CHEVROLET

Now even greater than the original in . . .

Looks and Performance!

▲ At the Daytona Beach Speed Week in January *(above)*, Corvette engineer Zora Arkus-Duntov took the wheel. In a two-way run Duntov averaged 150.583 mph. Note the cut-down windscreen, partially blocked grill, and knobby rear tires of the Daytona car *(top left)*.

◄ "Sensational to GO in. . . So smart to be SEEN in." So promised this brochure for this "true-blooded, tiger-tempered sports car" with "cat-sure cornering."

▲ A single, tall fin and faired-in head-rest marked the SR-2 show/race car.

▲ Handbuilt, the SR-2 powered through the flying mile at 152.866-mph.

▲ Chevrolet head Ed Cole sits at the wheel of a second, milder SR-2.

▲ Most Corvettes were two-toned, though some buyers pre-ferred single-color. Dual exhausts exited at fender tips, and the license was now at bumper level. The optional power top had to be partly collapsed before pressing the fold button.

▲ Corvettes could be ordered with a soft top or optional lift-off hardtop. Fiberglass construction was ideal for low-volume production and kept weight down. Dr. Dick Thompson's SCCA race wins helped boost the car's image.

▲ Drivers still had a hard time watching the tach, mounted at the center. Waffle-patterned vinyl upholstery was new.

▲ Twin air cleaners demonstrated the presence of a high-output version of the 265-cid V-8, blasting out 225 or 240 bhp. Corvette's brochure promised "whip-lash acceleration."

◀ With a single carburetor, the V-8 developed 210 horsepower—15 more than in 1955. Enlarged and hopped-up regularly, this basic engine would power Chevrolets for years to come.

ENGINE SPECS
1956

Type:	ohv v-8	ohv V-8	ohv V-8
Bore X stroke (in.):	3.75 X 3.00	3.75 X 3.00	3.75 X 3.00
Displacement (ci):	265	265	265
Compression ratio:	9.25:1	9.25:1	10.3:1[1]
Horsepower @ rpm (bhp):	210 @ 5600	225 @ 5600	240 @ 5600
Torque @ rpm (lbs/feet):	270 @ 3200	270 @ 3600	270 @ 5200
Fuel Delivery:	1 X 4-bbl.	2 X 4-bbl.	2 X 4-bbl.
Transmission:	3-speed manual, Powerglide	3-speed manual, Powerglide	3-speed manual

[1]Duntov "High-Lift " cam

DIMENSIONS

Wheelbase (in.):	102.0
Overall length (in.):	168.0
Overall height (in.):	52.0
Overall width (in.):	70.5
Track front/rear (in.):	57/59.3
Curb weight (lbs):	3020

1957

Bolstered by money provided in the 1956 Federal Aid Highway Act, work began on the interstate highway system.

Of more significance, on October 4 the Soviet Union launched the first earth satellite, Sputnik I, and another on November 3. The U.S. responded on December 6, but the Vanguard rocket exploded after rising only a few feet from its Cape Canaveral launch site, damaging U.S. prestige.

Earlier, on August 29, the U.S. Congress approved a civil rights bill. In September, Arkansas Governor Orval Faubus barred nine blacks from entering a Little Rock high school. President Eisenhower sent federal troops, and the students went back to school.

Meanwhile, Jack Kerouac published *On the Road*, a beatnik journal.

•Fuel injection is offered as an option on the Corvette and regular Chevys

•V-8 engine enlarged to 283 cubic inches; highest horse-power rating jumps to 283

•Four-speed manual gearbox introduced at mid-year

•Corvette output spurts upward nearly 83 percent

•Thunderbird sales still way ahead of Corvette's by more than three-to-one

•Ford beats Chevy in the annual production race

•National economy begins to falter

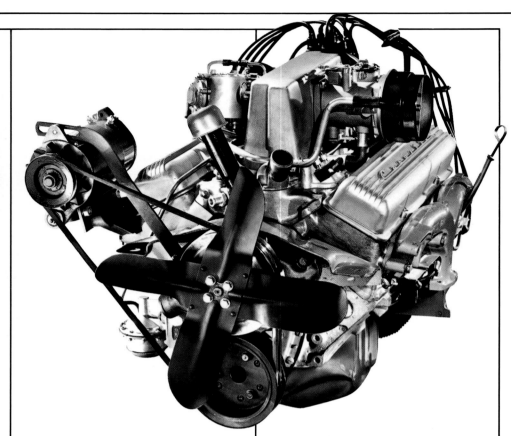

▲ With Ramjet Fuel Injection, Chevy's new 283-cid V-8 cranked out 250 or 283 horses. Solid lifters and a compression ratio of 10.5:1 helped the hottest version achieve a magic "1 h.p. per cu. in." However, reliability problems plagued the system.

"UND SO HELFE MIR, HERMANN, I WAS HOLDING 5900 R.P.M. AND HE CAME PAST ME LIKE A STUKA . . . AND PLAYING THE RADIO, TOO!"

CORVETTE
by Chevrolet

▲ Chevrolet promoted its competition successes and the "authentic" international character of this "real American sports car," noting that it "has given some distinguished visitors a rude shock." Americans liked its comforts, too.

▲ Zora Arkus-Duntov *(right)* and *Mechanix Illustrated* road tester Tom McCahill inspect Ramjet setup.

▲ Ramjet Fuel Injection—a "first" for volume production cars—undergoes testing in the fuel-flow room.

▲ Chevrolet's use of fiberglass kept Corvette weight down and, due to lower tooling costs, was ideal for low-volume production. In addition, fewer pieces were needed for assembly.

▲ Not until Studebaker's Avanti of 1962 would another major automaker use fiberglass for body construction. This year's 'Vette came in a wide choice of single- and two-tone colors.

▲ ▶The '57 Super Sport (or SS) show car was a mildly customized standard 'Vette with fuel-injection, four-speed gearbox, and heavy-duty racing suspension. A low "double-bubble" windscreen and forward-facing air scoops decorated the exterior.

▲ GM designer Bill Mitchell poses with the SR-2, set up for racing. Note the disc wheel covers and the faired-in headrest that extended into a tall fin. In bad weather, a transparent canopy was used. At times, cove air scoops were installed.

▲ Ideas for 1956-57 ranged from sublime to bizarre. This February 1955 proposal had partly exposed front wheels, like the Buick Wildcat II show car. The bullet-nose front was stranger yet; only the coves wound up on actual 'Vettes.

► Gauges still stretched across the Corvette dashboard, making at-a-glance readings somewhat difficult. The four-speed manual transmission became available at mid-year, to please enthusiasts who weren't content with three ratios or Powerglide automatic.

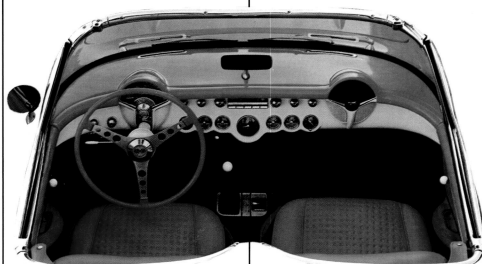

1957 Selected Colors

Onyx Black

Aztec Copper Met.

Cascade Green Met.

Arctic Blue

► Styling changed little for '57, but the price rose to $3465 and production hit 6339. Two-tone colors took full advantage of the pleasing cove contours. Buyers chose a fabric top (power optional) or $215 lightweight removable hardtop.

DIMENSIONS

Wheelbase (in.):	102
Overall length (in.):	168
Overall height (in.):	51.1
Overall width (in.):	70.5
Track front/rear (in.):	57/59
Curb weight (lbs):	2985

ENGINE SPECS

1957	Std.	RPO 469A	RPO 579A	RPO 469B	RPO 579B, E
Type:	ohv V-8	ohv V-8	ohv V-8	ohv V-8	ohv V-8
Bore X stroke (in.):	3.875 X 3.00	3.875 X 3.00	3.875 X 3.00	3.875 X 3.00	3.875 X 3.00
Displacement (ci):	283	283	283	283	283
Compression ratio:	9.5:1	9.5:1	9.5:1	9.5:1	10.5:1[1]
Horsepower @ rpm (bhp):	220 @ 4800	245 @ 5000	250 @ 5000	270 @ 6000	283 @ 6200
Torque @ rpm (lbs/feet):	300 @ 3000	300 @ 3800	305 @ 3800	285 @ 4200	290 @ 4400
Fuel Delivery:	1 X 4-bbl.	2 X 4-bbl.	Ramjet Fuel Injection	2 X 4-bbl.	Ramjet Fuel Injection
Transmission:	3- or 4-speed manual, Powerglide	3- or 4-speed manual, Powerglide	3- or 4-speed manual, Powerglide	3- or 4-speed manual	3- or 4-speed manual

[1]Duntov "High-Lift" cam

▲ Similarities to a stock or modestly-modified Corvette were most evident from the front, but the SR-2 looked far more aggressive with its longer snout and wider, "toothier" grille. A number of chassis/drivetrain elements were borrowed from the specially-built Sebring SS (see following section).

▲ Headlight domes and white scallops made the racing SR-2 easy to spot as it got last-minute attention. In addition to the aero-look "shark" fin behind the driver, the SR-2 sported huge chromed air scoops in body coves for this outing.

▲ Like other racing Corvettes, the SR-2 was impressive. In addition to running 16th at Sebring, it performed well at the 1957 Daytona Speed Weeks, where Buck Baker did a 93.047-mph standing mile and 152.866-mph flying mile.

▲ Racing activities under official Chevrolet auspices were only part of the picture—and less so after the Automobile Manufacturers Association banned factory competition at mid-year.

▲ All Corvette engines for '57 grew to 283-cid, whether carbureted or fuel-injected. The base V-8 delivered 220 bhp, but twin four-barrel carbs (above) helped raise output to 245 horsepower.

◄ Ads insisted that "the driver who has whipped the Corvette through a series of S-turns really knows the facts of life: This sleek powerhouse handles!" Purists disdained fake knock-off hubs.

▲ By 1957, the Corvette had evolved into a true race-and-ride machine. Suspension touch-ups brought handling that even Europeans were forced to respect.

▼ Priced at $450, Ramjet Fuel Injection proved troublesome. Only about 1040 '57s had it (756 with the 283-bhp rating). With 283 bhp, 0-60 took just over six seconds. Fuzzy dice were popular add-ons.

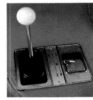

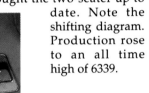

◀▼ Holes in the steering wheel helped add a competitive touch to the Corvette. Arrival of the four-speed gearbox brought the two-seater up to date. Note the shifting diagram. Production rose to an all time high of 6339.

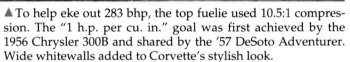

▲ To help eke out 283 bhp, the top fuelie used 10.5:1 compression. The "1 h.p. per cu. in." goal was first achieved by the 1956 Chrysler 300B and shared by the '57 DeSoto Adventurer. Wide whitewalls added to Corvette's stylish look.

▲ Though fuel injection added glamour to the Corvette's image, this car has the lower-status three-speed manual gearbox—perhaps because the four-speed didn't appear until mid-year. Note the attractive waffle-pattern vinyl bucket seats. Power windows (not seen here) were optional.

▶ Made by GM's Rochester Carburetor Division, constant-flow mechanical fuel injection was designed mainly by the GM Engineering Staff. A special two-piece aluminum manifold casting was used on the hottest V-8.

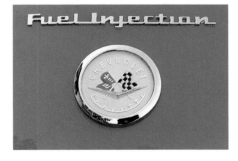

◀ Fuel-injected 'Vettes got special badging and cost the buyer an extra $450 to $675.

1957 Corvette SS

New Chevy general manager Ed Cole believed in the maxim, "Race on Sunday, Sell on Monday." Racing success would boost Corvette's image. Thus the Super Sport.

Developed as project XP-64, the Corvette SS was built for racing at Sebring in 1957. The dramatic racer sported a long bullet-style headrest and used a space frame to save weight.

Though fast and powerful, the car clearly needed more development. Its Sebring trial ended after 23 laps and a series of mechanical woes. Soon, the manufacturers' ban on racing cut short its life.

▲ Zora Arkus-Duntov inspects a brake drum, one of many unique SS components. Two-leading shoe brakes replaced the usual duo-servo units.

▲ Duntov and other engineers worked long hours at Chevrolet's Engineering Center to make the SS race-ready. Sebring was second only to Le Mans in the hierarchy of international racing events.

▲ Styling, although heavily influenced by the D-Type racing Jaguar, looked more like production 1956 'Vettes. By the time the grill was added to the full-size clay, the resemblance was clear.

▲ As part of its development, the SS underwent wind-tunnel tests in December 1956. Sheet magnesium formed the body.

▲ The SS was distinguished by a long bullet-style headrest, hidden head-lamps, modified side "coves," and an elongated snout, seen here in a September 1956 mock-up.

▲ Wind-tunnel testing of the Super Sport revealed that lift was moderate and drag about the same as with the D-Type Jag.

▲ A tubular space frame of chrome-moly steel was used, with de Dion rear axle and '56 Chrysler Center-Plane front drums. Rears were mounted inboard.

▲ The transmission case was made of aluminum to save weight, which was a major concern in overall SS design.

◄ Moving closer to completion, the de Dion axle was curved to go around the Halibrand quick-change differential.

▲ Both the front and rear bodywork lifted up and away for servicing. Here, the SS, which weighed just 1850 pounds and rode a 72-inch wheelbase (30 inches shorter than stock), was nearing completion. Note the side exhausts. Coves got detachable covers.

▲ The SS is shown lapping the track at Sebring. Though ill-fated that day, it's fondly recalled as a symbol of Chevy ingenuity.

▶ Down-to-business interior featured thin-shell bucket seats and full gauges, including huge tach and novel mirror.

▲ Zora Arkus-Duntov studies the heart of the "Sebring SS." The fuel-injected, 283-cid V-8 yielded 307 bhp at 6400 rpm. Variable-rate coil springs were used up front.

▲ Prior to its Sebring outing, the SS had recorded an amazing 183 mph at GM's Mesa, Arizona, proving grounds. Note the exposed exhaust system.

▲ At long last, the finished Super Sport is rolled out the shop door, ready to head toward the Sebring race course in Florida for the March 1957 event. The SS raced in the prototype class.

▲ A plastic top was devised to meet varying rules, some of which called for a roof on every car entered. Note hood straps and tubular steel exhaust, which saved weight and added about 20 bhp.

◀ Problems came quickly at the Sebring 12-Hour Race, led by erratic brakes and flat-spotted tires. The coil had to be replaced; then the rear suspension acted up. The SS retired after 23 laps. Here the SS chases a D-Type Jaguar and another 'Vette.

▲ Running at Sebring in 1957, the SS had its exhaust pipe partly exposed. Though success was elusive, it remains one of the most intriguing cars in GM history.

America suffered the worst recession of the postwar. Explorer I, America's first successful satellite, was launched in January, as the first nuclear powerplant went online.

During an 18-day visit to Latin America in May, Vice-President Nixon faced hostile mobs in Peru and Venezuela. Five thousand Marines went to Lebanon after an Iraqi coup and internal turmoil.

Pan American World Airways initiated the first U.S. jet service to Europe. The price of a stamp rose from three to six cents.

Elvis Presley was drafted into the Army in March. To the distress of New York's baseball fans, both the Giants and Dodgers moved to California. John Keats published an amusing yet scathing indictment of the auto industry, *The Insolent Chariots.*

• Despite added size and weight, and quad headlamps, Corvette shows little change

• V-8 engine enlarged to 283 cubic inches; highest horsepower rating jumps to 283

• Styling doodads include dummy cove scoops, fake hood louvers, and decklid trim

• Production jumps to an impressive 9168 Corvettes

• Ford Thunderbird is transformed into personal-luxury four-seater

• GM marks its 50th anniversary of incorporation

In repose before Palm Springs' exclusive Racquet Club, or in action under the California desert sun, Corvette has proved itself the peer of the world's finest production sports cars.

WHEREVER THE WORLD'S BEST SPORTS CARS GATHER

CORVETTE DOES AMERICA PROUD!
by Chevrolet

A great sports car is not made overnight. It is developed and refined through years of testing and competition, until its handling becomes silk-smooth, its roadability flawless, its cyclonic power tempered to absolute reliability under the harshest demands.

Such a car is today's Corvette—a road machine that has won absolute respect abroad for its unique blend of docility and stunning performance, of elegant luxury and incredible roadholding.

It is our belief that a Corvette can provide you with more pleasure per mile of road than any other sports car in the world today. That is a bold assertion—but the proof is easy. See your Chevrolet dealer in the next day or so and arrange a road trial. Five minutes behind the wheel and you'll know!
. . . Chevrolet Division of General Motors, Detroit 2, Michigan.

▲ Corvette was touted as an *international* sports car—but with uniquely American virtues. In addition to top road manners, 'Vettes were rugged and easy to service.

◄ Wearing new quad headlights and with easy-to-read instruments inside, Corvette was billed as a dual-purpose machine. The car was "as American as the Fourth of July . . . a red-white-and-blue-blooded sportsman [but] also the leisure car supreme." Customers were treated to a "comfortable tourer, rally car, trials car . . . at one and the same time."

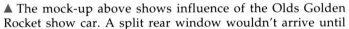

▲ The mock-up above shows influence of the Olds Golden Rocket show car. A split rear window wouldn't arrive until '63. With pointy fins and bullet rear bumpers, this 'Vette would have been quite a change from prior generations *(top)*.

ENGINE SPECS

1958	Std.	RPO 469	RPO 579	RPO469C	RPO579D
Type:	ohv V-8	ohv V-8	ohv V-8	ohv V-8	ohv V-8
Bore X stroke (in.):	3.875 X 3.00	3.875 X 3.00	3.875 X 3.00	3.875 X 3.00	3.875 X 3.00
Displacement (ci):	283	283	283	283	283
Compression ratio:	9.5:1	9.5:1	9.5:1	10.5:1[1]	10.5:1[1]
Horsepower @ rpm (bhp):	230 @ 4800	245 @ 5000	250 @ 5000	270 @ 6000	290 @ 6200
Torque @ rpm (lbs/feet):	300 @ 3000	300 @ 3800	305 @ 3800	285 @ 4200	290 @ 4400
Fuel Delivery:	1 X 4-bbl.	2 X 4-bbl.	Ramjet Fuel Injection	2 X 4-bbl.	Ramjet Fuel Injection
Transmission:	3- or 4-speed manual, Powerglide	3- or 4-speed manual, Powerglide	3- or 4-speed manual, Powerglide	3- or 4-speed manual	3- or 4-speed manual

[1]Duntov "High-Lift" cam

▲ By January 1956, the general shape was fixed, including quad headlights, but a mesh grille was still under consideration.

▲ Rear end styling for '58 was close to final by early 1956, including decklid chrome. Bumper styles were uncertain.

▲ A fresh grille was evolving. Except for details, this February 1956 creation was close to the finished '58 design.

▲ Modest rear revisions included reshaped exhaust outlets. Vent-like extractors in coves weren't yet formed.

▲ This hardtop mock-up for '58 looks almost ready to roll out the door. Cove revisions had yet to be determined.

DIMENSIONS

Wheelbase (in.):	102
Overall length (in.):	177.2
Overall height (in.):	51.1
Overall width (in.):	72.8
Track front/rear (in.):	57/59
Curb weight (lbs):	3050

▲ Bodyside coves carried over from the prior generation, but three trim strips were used to accent simulated vents. Fender script reveals that this car has a $484 fuel-injected 283-cid V-8. Top fuelie was upped to 290 bhp at 6200 rpm. Other engines offered 230 to 250 horsepower.

◄ Styling of the 1958 Corvette was obviously evolutionary. Although the rear end was the least changed element, it sported revised (but still slim) bumpers and oval exhaust outlets, new taillight lenses, and twin chrome strips on the decklid.

1958 Selected Colors

Charcoal

Snowcrest White

Silver Blue

Regal Turquoise

Panama Yellow

Signet Red

▲ Virtually any scenic site could highlight the lines of the latest 'Vette. Wraparound bumpers looked hardly more protective than earlier versions, but they were now attached to the frame and complemented the clean profile.

◄ Even the '58 'Vette was caught up in GM's corporate chrome extravaganza. Dual exhaust tips had a neatly integrated appearance, but decklid trim and fake air vents in fender coves weren't appreciated by the motor media. Neither were the simulated hood louvers.

▼ This year's grille had nine teeth, compared to 13 in '57. The glitzy front end included dummy air scoops alongside the grille, plus chrome bezels around the quad headlights. Because the full-size Chevrolets were all-new for 1958, Corvettes received only modest attention.

▲ Two-tone color schemes, with contrasting coves, remained popular. Base price was $3631, and 9168 were built.

▲ A revised interior put instruments ahead of the driver and included a passenger assist bar. "Wonder Bar" radio cost $144.

Fidel Castro's rebel troops ousted Cuban dictator Fulgencio Batista, and the U.S. recognized the new government in January. Alaska and Hawaii became the 49th and 50th states—the first additions since Arizona in 1912. In June, the St. Lawrence Seaway opened, linking the Great Lakes with the Atlantic Ocean.

While visiting an American model kitchen at an exhibit in Moscow, Soviet Premier Khrushchev and Vice-President Nixon exchanged heated words. Later that year, Khrushchev toured the United States. Charles Van Doren admitted that he'd received answers in advance on *Twenty-One*, a TV quiz show. Also on the tube, Westerns were the big thing, and included *Bonanza* and *Rawhide*. Vance Packard's book, *The Status Seekers*, dissected the American class structure.

Rock singers Buddy Holly, Ritchie Valens and the "Big Bopper" (J.P. Richardson) died in a plane crash.

• Corvette styling smooths out, as hood louvers and deck trim are deleted

• Gearshift lever gets a lockout T-handle; anti-fade brakes and nylon-cord tires become available

• Corvette production edges upward to 9670

• Chevy and Ford end year in near dead-heat, each making more than 1.4 million cars

• Federal gas tax rises from 3 to 4 cents per gallon

▲ Interior changes for '59 included repositioned door handles and armrests, reshaped seats with more lateral support, and a storage bin under the passenger grab bar (now padded). The tachometer was now directly ahead of the driver.

CORVETTE, '59 EDITION

by Chevrolet

NEW SLEEKNESS, ELEGANCE AND ROADABILITY FOR AMERICA'S ONLY SPORTS CAR!

Take a great basic design. Give its creators time to polish and refine every facet of its behavior—and you can come up with a classic road machine like the new Corvette.

Every change made for 1959 contributes new precision, new performance, new pleasure to what is admittedly the greatest driver's car produced in this country. Everything, from the superior traction of the new rear suspension to the deeper "bucket" contour of the seats to the cooling air slots in the wheel discs, is designed from the pilot's point of view.

Corvette, quite literally, offers a completely different dimension in road travel. If you haven't driven any Corvette yet, we can promise you a genuinely astonishing afternoon. But, even if you have experienced earlier versions, even if you are now a Corvette owner, we urge this: Try the '59 edition—you, too, can be profoundly impressed! ... Chevrolet Division of General Motors, Detroit 2, Michigan.

▲ New features promoted by Chevrolet included the radius-rod rear suspension and deeper "bucket" seats, plus cooling slots in wheel covers. Cleaned-up styling deleted the chrome trunk straps and hood louvers that were criticized in 1958.

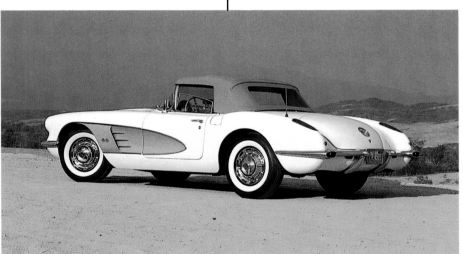

▲ Two-tone paint jobs remained popular, such as this Snowcrest White convertible with Inca Silver coves. Despite minimal change, Chevy promised that the 'Vette "reaches a new peak of performance and responsiveness . . . Fresh styling joins with suspension, brake, and power improvements to maintain the Corvette as America's top sports car."

◄ Whether in convertible form or with the $236.75 detachable hardtop, the '59 'Vette was a looker—America's most exotic production car. Many fans bought one for appearance alone. Triple windsplits remained in coves. Nylon-cord tires became available.

▲ Though far from cavernous, trunk space wasn't bad for a genuine sports car. Production rose to a record 9670 units, despite a 7-percent price hike to $3875. Note the slim wraparound bumpers. Inside the cockpit, dual sunvisors cost extra.

▲ Most popular of the 283-cid engines was the basic 230-horsepower version, with a single carburetor. Only 1092 enthusiasts chose fuel injection. Of those, 920 got the hot 290-bhp edition, whose 0-60 dashes took seven seconds or less.

▲ GM design chief Bill Mitchell's XP-87 Stingray race/show car rode the same chassis as the 1957 SS. Though it took some styling ques from the never-produced Q-Corvette, the dazzling racer was "privately" run by Mitchell.

▲ Flaunting a slim oval grille housed in an aggressively protruding snout, Bill Mitchell's XP-700 show car belied its Corvette basis. Kinship was more evident toward the rear, which may have inspired the back end of the production 1961.

▲ With racecar driver Phil Hill seated behind the wheel, Bill Mitchell stands beside his race-ready Stingray Special. The basic shape of the Stingray was refined by stylist Larry Shinoda. This racing Stingray led directly to the XP-755 Shark show car.

DIMENSIONS

Wheelbase (in.):	102
Overall length (in.):	177.2
Overall height (in.):	52
Overall width (in.):	72.8
Track front/rear (in.):	57/59
Curb weight (lbs)	3080

ENGINE SPECS

1959	Std.	RPO 269	RPO 579	RPO 469C	RPO 579D
Type:	ohv V-8	ohv V-8	ohv V-8	ohv V-8	ohv V-8
Bore X stroke (in.):	3.875 X 3.00	3.875 X 3.00	3.875 X 3.00	3.875 X 3.00	3.875 X 3.00
Displacement (ci):	283	283	283	283	283
Compression ratio:	9.5:1	9.5:1	9.5:1	10.5:1[1]	10.5:1[1]
Horsepower @ rpm (bhp):	230 @ 4800	245 @ 5000	250 @ 5000	270 @ 6000	290 @ 6200
Torque @ rpm (lbs/feet):	300 @ 3000	300 @ 3800	305 @ 3800	285 @ 4200	290 @ 4400
Fuel Delivery:	1 X 4-bbl.	2 X 4-bbl.	Ramjet Fuel Injection	2 X 4-bbl.	Ramjet Fuel Injection
Transmission:	3- or 4-speed manual, Powerglide	3- or 4-speed manual, Powerglide	3- or 4-speed manual, Powerglide	3- or 4-speed manual	3- or 4-speed manual

[1]Duntov "High-Lift" cam

▲ Transformed from private racer into an official Chevy show car, not much of the Stingray's looks carried over into the '58-

'62 'Vettes. However, it is clear that this car was a precursor of the production 1963 Sting Ray.

▲ Campaigned by private owners, Corvettes proved their valor. Chevrolet had backed away from racing in 1957, but Mitchell's Stingray remained active. At Meadowdale Raceway the 'Ray leads a Chaparral and trio of Porsche Spyder 1500s.

▲ Late in 1959, the Stingray Special goes through its paces. Initially red, it was later repainted silver.

▲ The Stingray Special, here at Laguna Seca, is trailed by "The Terror of the West Coast," a Type 61 Bird Cage Maserati. Dr. Dick Thompson won the C-Modified championship in 1959 and '60.

▲ Despite front-end damage, the Stingray kept rolling. Giving chase is 'Ol Yeller II, a West Coast special created by Max Balchowsky and tested by Dan Gurney. Given the AMA's ban on racing, the Sting Ray could not race as a Chevrolet.

This year's Census calculated that the population of the U.S. neared 180 million. Non-violent "sit-ins" began in the South, to protest racial discrimination.

Soviet aircraft downed an American U-2 spy plane over Soviet territory and captured its pilot, Francis Gary Powers. The first nuclear-powered aircraft carrier, the *Enterprise,* was launched—it was the world's longest ship.

Massachusetts Senator John F. Kennedy defeated former Vice-President Richard Nixon for the presidency.

TV journalist Edward R. Murrow chronicled the plight of migratory farm workers in *Harvest of Shame.* Chubby Checker recorded "The Twist," starting a new dance craze.

•Corvette is largely a carryover, but with more aluminum parts and new front/rear stabilizer bars

•More than half of the 10,261 Corvettes built this year come with four-speed manual transmissions

•Corvette buyers get five choices for the 283-cid V-8, from 230 to 315 horsepower

•Rear-engined Corvair debuts as Chevrolet's compact entry

•Chevrolet displays XP-700 experimental Corvette

•Three Corvettes enter 24 Hours of Le Mans race

•National Auto Show held at Detroit's new Cobo Hall

▲ Appearance changes for 1960 were minimal, but engineering improvements gave the top two fuel-injected engines some extra power. A larger-diameter front anti-roll bar and new rear bar created a smoother ride and more neutral handling.

▲ Chevrolet continued to promote the Corvette's dual image, as a tourer and as a performance machine. Customers obviously bought the concept, as production edged up to 10,261. Not too many had the top $484.20, 315-bhp engine.

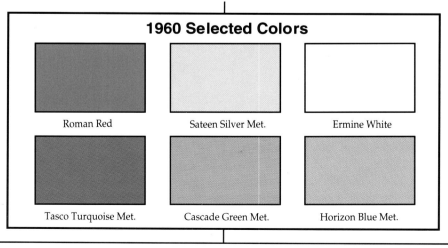

1960 Selected Colors

Roman Red	Sateen Silver Met.	Ermine White
Tasco Turquoise Met.	Cascade Green Met.	Horizon Blue Met.

▲ Standard blackwalls and small hub-caps gave a down-to-business look. Serious drivers even skipped radio or heater.

▶ With solid valve lifters and 11.0:1 compression, the top fuelie delivered 315 bhp (up from 290) at 6200 rpm.

Fuel Injection

▼ For '59 the close-ratio four-speed manual had a new, lightweight aluminum clutch housing. At $188, it went into over half of production.

ENGINE SPECS

1960	Std.	RPO 469	RPO 469C	RPO 579	RPO 579D
Type:	ohv V-8	ohv V-8	ohv V-8	ohv V-8	ohv V-8
Bore X stroke (in.):	3.875 X 3.00	3.875 X 3.00	3.875 X 3.00	3.875 X 3.00	3.875 X 3.00
Displacement (ci):	283	283	283	283	283
Compression ratio:	9.5:1	9.5:1	10.5:1[1]	11.0:1	11.0:1[1]
Horsepower @ rpm (bhp):	230 @ 4800	245 @ 5000	270 @ 6000	275 @ 5200	315 @ 6200
Torque @ rpm (lbs/feet):	300 @ 3000	300 @ 3800	285 @ 4200	290 @ 4200	295 @ 5100
Fuel Delivery:	1 X 4-bbl.	2 X 4-bbl.	2 X 4-bbl.	Ramjet Fuel Injection	Ramjet Fuel Injection
Transmission:	3- or 4-speed manual, Powerglide	3- or 4-speed manual, Powerglide	3- or 4-speed manual	3- or 4-speed manual	3- or 4-speed manual

[1]Duntov "High-Lift " cam

DIMENSIONS

Wheelbase (in.):	102
Overall length (in.):	177.2
Overall height (in.):	52.3
Overall width (in.):	72.8
Track front/rear (in.):	57/59

▶ Those familiar grille "teeth" were in their final season. On TV, actors Martin Milner and George Maharis began to roam *Route 66* in a current Corvette.

▼ Hard to be sure at a glance that this luscious 'Vette is a '60. Base price dropped $3, to $3872. Optional, power operated top cost $140.

▲ The mildest of the 283-cid V-8s was again rated 230 horsepower, with a single four-barrel carburetor. Stepping up to twin four-barrels brought 245 bhp or, with high-lift cam, 270 bhp. A subtler fuelie with hydraulic lifters made 275 bhp.

◄ Little was new inside the Corvette, with its deep-contoured bucket seats, competition type steering wheel, and gauges located ahead of the driver. Note the color-coordinated seatbelts, which had been available in Corvettes since 1958.

▼ Contrasting-color bodyside coves remained popular, and kept their triple windsplit spears. Note the curious rise of the roll-up windows—one of the Corvette's quirks. New options included a thermostatic cooling fan and 24-gallon gas tank.

Before leaving office in January, President Eisenhower uttered his oft-repeated warning about "unwarranted influence by the military-industrial complex." In his inaugural address, President Kennedy told Americans to "Ask not what your country can do for you. Ask what you can do for your country."

Kennedy launched the Peace Corps in March. A month later came the disastrous "Bay of Pigs" invasion into Cuba.

In May, 400 Green Beret troops and 100 advisers were sent to Vietnam, adding to the 2000 advisers already in that country. "Freedom Riders" were attacked in the South during segregation protests.

Alan B. Shepard Jr. became the first American in space, shooting 115 miles upward in a Mercury capsule.

• "Ducktail" Corvette rear end from XP-700 show car holds four round taillamps

• Chrome mesh screen replaces familiar tooth-style grille

• Standard-equipment list expands—but heater is extra

• Narrowed transmission tunnel boosts passenger space

• Production grows slightly, to 10,939 two-seaters with choice of five V-8 ratings

• 315-bhp fuel-injected V-8 can send a Corvette to 60 mph in a snappy 5.5 seconds

▲ Evolved from the Stingray racer and XP-700 show car, '61's new "ducktail" rear end sported small round taillights on each side of a central license-plate recess.

▲ Bill Mitchell's XP-700 had a protruding loop-style bumper/grille that never saw production. Its simple, flowing rear end evolved into the '61 "ducktail."

▲ For '61 the vertical-toothed grille and chrome headlight bezels were gone.

▲ A modest trunklid crease ran through the traditional round emblem.

▲ Most buyers paid $16.15 for contrasting-color coves in their final year. Also optional: direct-flow exhaust (no charge) and a heavy-duty suspension ($333.60).

▲ Although Bill Mitchell had plenty of ideas for restyling, the new Corvair and Chevy II were Chevrolet priorities in the early '60s. With its de-chromed makeover, the 1961-62 editions ranked as best the 'Vettes since the "classic" '57. Mechanical improvements took precedence, and fit/finish was the best yet. For the first time, dual exhausts exited below the body.

▲ In addition to clean lines, the "duck-tail" rear end added 20 percent more luggage space. Chrome bumperettes bracketed the license plate, which gained a small "arched" bumper.

▶ Both the dashboard and interior were virtually unchanged. Shoppers didn't seem to mind, because at 10,939 units, the '61 set another production record.

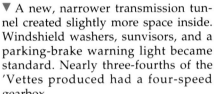

▼ A new, narrower transmission tunnel created slightly more space inside. Windshield washers, sunvisors, and a parking-brake warning light became standard. Nearly three-fourths of the 'Vettes produced had a four-speed gearbox.

▲ The new rear-quarter creaseline began at the rear wheel openings. Coves now displayed a rectangular nameplate with red and blue hash marks. Despite its lacking an independent rear suspension, the Corvette was now a world class road car.

▲ A fine horizontal mesh grille with body-color headlight bezels marked the freshened 'Vette. A crossed-flags emblem, above separate letters spelling out the car name, replaced the former round emblem. Base price rose $62, to $3934.

▲ A power top was optional, and a heater added $102.25. Standard gear now included a thermostatic fan and aluminum radiator.

1961 Selected Colors

Roman Red	Ermine White
Honduras Maroon Met.	Jewel Blue Met.
Fawn Beige Met.	

DIMENSIONS

Wheelbase (in.):	102
Overall length (in.):	176.7
Overall height (in.):	52.9
Overall width (in.):	70.4
Track front/rear (in.):	57/59
Curb weight (lbs):	3108

ENGINE SPECS

1961	Std.	RPO 469	RPO 468	RPO 353	RPO 354
Type:	ohv V-8	ohv V-8	ohv V-8	ohv V-8	ohv V-8
Bore X stroke (in.):	3.875 X 3.00	3.875 X 3.00	3.875 X 3.00	3.875 X 3.00	3.875 X 3.00
Displacement (ci):	283	283	283	283	283
Compression ratio:	9.5:1	9.5:1	10.5:1[1]	11.0:1	11.0:1[1]
Horsepower @ rpm (bhp):	230 @ 4800	245 @ 5000	270 @ 6000	275 @ 5200	315 @ 6200
Torque @ rpm (lbs/feet):	300 @ 3000	300 @ 3000	285 @ 4200	290 @ 4200	295 @ 5100
Fuel Delivery:	1 X 4-bbl.	2 X 4-bbl.	2 X 4-bbl.	Ramjet Fuel Injection	Ramjet Fuel Injection
Transmission:	3- or 4-speed manual, Powerglide	3- or 4-speed manual, Powerglide	3- or 4-speed manual	3- or 4-speed manual	3- or 4-speed manual

[1]Duntov "High-Lift" cam

1962

In February, astronaut John Glenn became the first American to orbit the earth. The U.S. Supreme Court banned prayers in public schools.

The Cuban Missile Crisis ended on October 28. After a week of extreme tension, Soviet Premier Khrushchev agreed to remove the missiles that had been installed on the island-nation.

The drug thalidomide was banned in the U.S. following European reports of birth defects among children of women who had taken it. A Telstar satellite relayed TV signals to earth for the first time.

Defeated in a race for California governor and angry with the press, Richard Nixon announced that "You won't have Nixon to kick around any more." James Meredith became the first black student at the University of Mississippi.

• Corvette sales set record, with 14,531 built

• Two-tone paint jobs no longer offered on Corvettes

• New 327-cid V-8 delivers as much as 360 horsepower when fuel-injected

• New experimental cars in '62 include Chevrolet's CERV-I

• Shelby American Inc. begins production of its Cobra-based model

• Studebaker launches fiberglass-bodied Avanti

• GM installs the first industrial robots

corvette
FOR 1962

NON-MECHANICAL MEN ARISE!

There's a cult of sports-car-type people who spread the myth that one needs vast knowledge of things mechanical to own a sports car. Be not deceived! This may be true of some machines, but not the Corvette. Any Corvette, however equipped, will give unruffled, unfussy driving pleasure while outperforming cars that cost three times as much and require the full-time attention of a bilingual mechanic. No, friends, if you yearn to spend long hours lying on cold cement, covered with grease, shop elsewhere. Corvettes are for driving; fill them with gas and people and point them down the road. That's the way to enjoy this automobile! Of course, if you simply must do something, we don't mind if you wash it yourself. (Radio, as shown, optional at extra cost.) . . . Chevrolet Division of General Motors, Detroit 2, Mich.

CORVETTE BY CHEVROLET

▲ Even cleaner looking than '61, Corvette kept its big news underhood: a 327-cid V-8. Mesh grille and flanking cutouts were black-out.

◄ Rather than focusing on the mechanically adept, Corvette was pushed as a performance car that would "give unruffled, unfussy driving pleasure."

▲ This styling clay from January 13, 1959, reveals the general front-end shape, but grille medallion would disappear.

▲ Thick vertical cove slots would change considerably by production time, but the "ducktail" rear would be carried over.

▲ This February '59 mockup was never produced, but headlights and wraparound body crease suggest the '63 'Ray.

▲ Designers were pondering radical change in 1959. Beltline crease and fender vents aren't far removed from Sting Ray.

▲ Chevrolet didn't try to hide the inspiration for the XP-755 Shark show car's long snout and fender gills. Renamed Mako Shark I, it led to the '63 Sting Ray.

▲ Race driver Betty Skelton, shown at the wheel of a '62 Corvette, set a record for American sports cars at Daytona Beach in 1956, topping 150 mph.

ENGINE SPECS

1962	Std.	RPO 583	RPO 396	RPO 582
Type:	ohv V-8	ohv V-8	ohv V-8	ohv V-8
Bore X stroke (in.):	4.00 X 3.25	4.00 X 3.25	4.00 X 3.25	4.00 X 3.25
Displacement (ci):	327	327	327	327
Compression ratio:	10.5:1	10.5:1	11.25:1[1]	11.25:1[1]
Horsepower @ rpm (bhp):	250 @ 4400	300 @ 5000	340 @ 6000	360 @ 6000
Torque @ rpm (lbs/feet):	350 @ 2800	360 @ 3200	344 @ 4000	352 @ 4000
Fuel Delivery:	1 X 4-bbl.	1 X 4-bbl. (AFB)	1 X 4-bbl. (AFB)	Ramjet Fuel Injection
Transmission:	3- or 4-speed manual, Powerglide	3- or 4-speed manual, Powerglide	3- or 4-speed manual	3- or 4-speed manual

[1]Duntov "High-Lift " cam

▲ Not much change was evident, but the '62 looked more sophisticated with its single-color body paint and coves *sans* chromed surrounds. In their stead were black ribbed-aluminum appliqués.

▶ Interior changes were modest. This was the first Corvette with a standard heater.

▼ Chevrolet bored/stroked its V-8 to 327-cid displacement. Outputs ranged from 250 bhp all the way to a fuel-injected 360 bhp. That one roared from 0-60 in 5.9 seconds and ran the quarter in 14.5. Quicker and better handling than ever, the '62 was also more civilized—without losing the car's basic charm.

▲ Ending an era, the '62 lost the last of the '50's styling excesses and proved the most popular yet—output was 14,531. Narrow whitewalls were new.

1962 Selected Colors

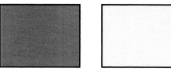

Roman Red

Almond Beige

Sateen Silver Met.

Ermine White

Honduras Maroon Met.

Fawn Beige Met.

▶ During the same race, the Don Yenko Corvette (No. 10) leads a Lister-Chevrolet (No. 8). Class B competition was dominated by the 283-cid cars of Yenko and Frank Dominianni.

▲ Rocker panels wore ribbed aluminum moldings—the only new decoration.

▲ Luggage space was still modest, so an optional truck rack was available.

DIMENSIONS

Wheelbase (in.):	102
Overall length (in.):	176.7
Overall height (in.):	52.9
Overall width (in.):	70.4
Track front/rear (in.):	57/59
Curb weight (lbs):	3137

◀ Don Yenko's Corvette is inspected at the Daytona 3-Hour Race. To its rear (No. 11) is Dr. Dick Thompson's car.

In a year of turmoil, the U.S. Supreme Court ruled that all criminal defendants must have counsel. In the summer, the U.S., Soviet Union, and Britain signed a nuclear test-ban treaty (except for underground testing). On August 28, Martin Luther King, Jr., uttered his famous "I have a dream..." speech before 200,000 civil rights demonstrators in Washington.

Tragically, President John F. Kennedy was assassinated on November 22 in Dallas; Vice-President Lyndon B. Johnson took his place.

Earlier that month, South Vietnamese president Ngo Dinh Diem had been assassinated. By year's end, the U.S. had 15,000 troops in Vietnam and spent $500 million in aid.

Postal ZIP codes debut. Arthur Ashe became the first black member of the U.S. Davis Cup tennis team.

• All-new Sting Ray debuts

• A unique split-rear-window coupe joins the convertible

• Split window criticized at the time, but coupe becomes one of the most coveted Corvettes

• Hidden headlights are the first on an American car since the 1942 DeSoto

• Industry sales climb 8.17 percent, and Corvette output leaps nearly 50 percent

• Grand Sport racing Corvette arrives; only five built before GM axes program

▲ By autumn 1959, the experimental XP-720 project was underway as the initial step in the Sting Ray design program. This prototype convertible is similar to the final version, but lacks headlights and has air vents ahead of the back wheels.

▲ GM design chief Bill Mitchell poses with his Stingray racer and the new Sting Ray coupe. He was largely responsible for designing both. The production Sting Ray was based extensively on the racing car—especially the humped fenders.

▲ A ³/₈-scale clay model of the emerging Sting Ray endures aerodynamic testing in the Cal Tech wind tunnel—a Corvette "first," and rare for any American car.

▲ Not only was the '63 all new, but it was also the first time the Corvette was available as a closed coupe. The coupe above is a pre-production model and has an experimental lift-back.

▲ A quality inspector carefully checks a Sting Ray coupe—one of 10,594 built—as the car nears the end of the assembly line.

▲ At the St. Louis assembly plant, an overhead conveyor lowers a coupe body onto its chassis.

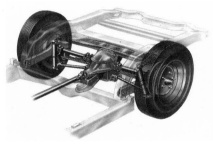

▲ Corvette engineer Zora Arkus-Duntov fought hard for independent rear suspension—and the Sting Ray got it.

▲ Overhead view of the coupe emphasizes its sleek aero look. Doors were cut into the roof for easier entry/exit.

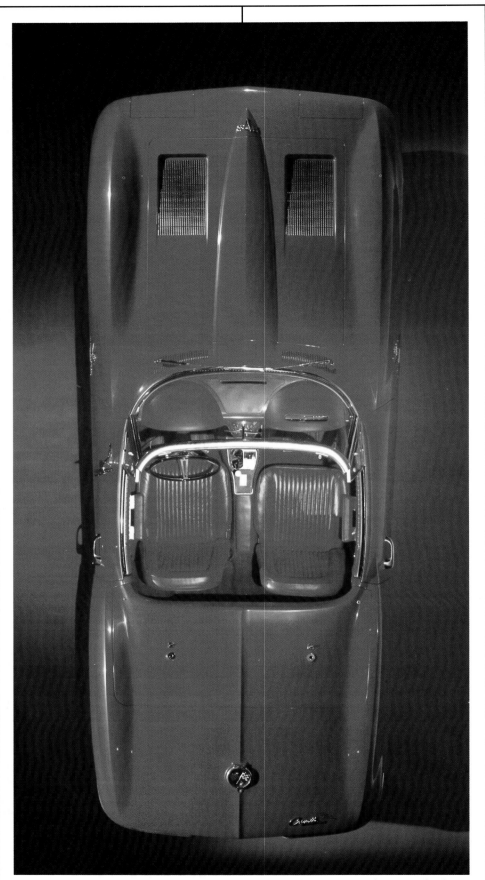

▲ The '63 was the first 'Vette to lack a decklid. Trunk access was from inside. Sting Ray wheelbase was 98 inches—four inches shorter than before. Coupled with quicker steering, that reduction aided maneuverability. At 175.2 inches the car was two inches shorter than before. Independent rear suspension consisted of a frame-mounted differential with U-joined halfshafts and a nineleaf transverse spring.

▲ Bodyside styling features included fake air extractor vents in the pillar—behind the doors—and ribbed rocker panels. The dummy vents brought jeers, and wouldn't last long.

▲ A total of 10,919 convertibles (still called a roadster, despite roll-up windows) were built. The old X-braced frame gave way to a ladder-type design with five cross members.

▲ Chevrolet considered a four-seat Sting Ray and created this extended-wheelbase prototype in January 1962.

◄ The four-seat prototype Corvette, in comparison to Ford's T-bird, looks downright captivating. Actual production likely would have diluted Corvette's sports car image.

▲ In July 1963, Chevrolet gathered an intriguing selection of Corvettes, both old and new, to promote the car's heritage— even though it was barely a decade old. Bill Mitchell and his Stingray are up front, ahead of the XP-700 show car.

▲ A Sting Ray convertible listed for $4037; the coupe cost $4252. A $236.75 removable hardtop blended top-down fun with the snugness of a coupe.

▶ Power brakes and steering were now available. At $421 only 278 'Vettes (1.2%) had optional air conditioning.

▼ A racing-style gas cap with crossed-flags insignia went on the deck, replacing the old bodyside fuel flap.

▲ Although initial reaction to the coupe was favorable, many criticized poor rearward vision and lack of a trunklid.

▲ The coupe's split window emphasized the ridge that ran down the roof. The window would be replaced in '64.

ENGINE SPECS

1963	Std.	L75	L76	L84
Type:	ohv V-8	ohv V-8	ohv V-8	ohv V-8
Bore X stroke (in.):	4.00 X 3.25	4.00 X 3.25	4.00 X 3.25	4.00 X 3.25
Displacement (ci):	327	327	327	327
Compression ratio:	10.5:1	10.5:1	11.25:1[1]	11.25:1[1]
Horsepower @ rpm (bhp):	250 @ 4400	300 @ 5000	340 @ 6000	360 @ 6000
Torque @ rpm (lbs/feet):	350 @ 2800	360 @ 3200	344 @ 4000	352 @ 4000
Fuel Delivery:	1 X 4-bbl.	1 X 4-bbl. (AFB)	1 X 4-bbl. (AFB)	Ramjet Fuel Injection
Transmission:	3- or 4-speed manual, Powerglide	3- or 4-speed manual, Powerglide	3- or 4-speed manual	3- or 4-speed manual

[1]Duntov "High-Lift " cam

▲ The Corvette was quickly becoming a more civilized car. Nineteen sixty-three ushered in power brakes and power steering as well as leather seats and air conditioning.

▲ Bill Mitchell had insisted upon the divided window. Sadly, some owners later "updated" their '63s with one-piece Plexiglas.

▲ Trunklids were a part of the past, never to return. Functional pillar vents had been planned for the coupe, but were abandoned because of high cost.

▲ Quad headlights dwelled in rotating housings which, when closed, matched the pointy new front end. Purists objected to all the phony vents, but customers liked the new style. This car really looked like it was whizzing along, even when at a standstill. The stylish humped hood was borrowed from the Stingray racer.

1963 Selected Colors

Sebring Silver Met.

Riverside Red

Ermine White

Silver Blue Met.

Saddle Tan Met.

Daytona Blue Met.

Tuxedo Black

DIMENSIONS

Wheelbase (in.):	98
Overall length (in.):	175.3
Overall height (in.):	49.8
Overall width (in.):	69.6
Track front/rear (in.):	56.3/57
Curb weight (lbs):	3150

NEW CORVETTE

▲ Inside was a new interpretation of the "twin-cowl" Corvette dash. More practical than before, it brought a glovebox with a proper door, plus an improved heater, a new cowl-ventilation system, and a full set of easy-to-read gauges—all dead ahead of the driver. A vertically positioned radio was located in the center console.

▲ Even those experts who faulted Sting Ray styling praised its performance and new, fully independent rear suspension.

▲ Harley Earl, former head of GM's Art and Colour Studio, drove this '63 Sting Ray coupe, pictured here at Cypress Gardens. It wasn't exactly stock, as evidenced by the modified fake air-extractor vent on the passenger side. Kelsey Hayes cast aluminum wheels were supposed to be available, but had problems with porousness.

▲ Just 199 Corvettes had the Z06 heavy-duty suspension. Only 50 (including this coupe) came with a 36-gallon tank and sintered metallic power brakes.

► Fuel injection continued as an option via the L84 package, which gave the 327-cid V-8 a 360-horsepower rating. It cost $430.40. Fuel injection badges went on fenders, including a red/white/blue band below the lettering.

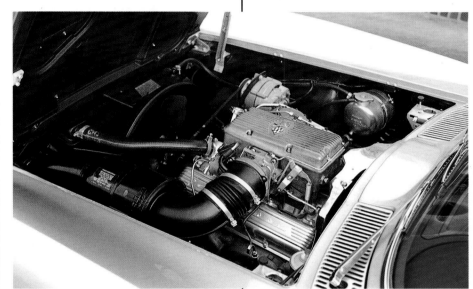

▲ Show cars continued to be a Corvette staple. This modification of a production convertible sports an eye-opening interior featuring white seats and trim appointments.

◄ This Corvette show car sported a web of side pipes exiting from the front quarter panels and ending just short of the rear wheels.

1963 Grand Sport

A lightweight, Sting Ray-based Grand Sport came to life because both Zora Arkus-Duntov and Chevrolet general manager Semon E. (Bunkie) Knudsen loved racing, and because Carroll Shelby's Ford-powered Cobra was running rings around Corvettes at the track. Work began in secret in 1962.

The car was tested at Sebring in December 1962, but GM's racing ban killed any hopes of real production—only five were built. Later, backed by private teams, the Grand Sports racked up impressive wins.

▲ Non-moving headlights behind Plexiglas covers and aggressive hood and rear scoops differentiate the GS from its lesser cousin. All told, there were three coupes and two roadsters.

▲ Though closely related to the production Sting Ray, the Grand Sport differed in nearly every element. The split rear window was deleted, and a small panel in the deck gave access to the spare tire. Note the side exhaust system.

▲ Suspension components were specially fabricated to help trim weight to 1900-2100 pounds. Disc brakes were 11.75-inch diameter British-built Girling units, with solid rotors and twin-piston aluminum calipers. Steering was ultra-quick.

▲ Although copying the Sting Ray, the GS was loaded with scoops.

▲ Hood tie-down buckles added to the Grand Sport's competitive look. A 36-gallon gas tank was added.

▲ The Grand Sport's fiberglass body was close to Sting Ray specs, but of thinner section and hand-laid. Underneath was the new ladder-type chassis, but with large tubular-steel side rails. Plexiglas side and rear windows were installed.

▲ Power came from a bored and stroked 377-cid enlargement of the small-block V-8, giving at least 550 bhp at 6400 rpm.

▶ Arkus-Duntov hoped for 125 Grand Sports, but only five were built before GM nixed the car. Each fell into private hands. Note quick-fill fuel inlet on the sail panel.

▲ Interiors featured one-piece molded bucket seats and serious instruments that included a 200-mph speedometer.

▲ Auxiliary gauges and switches for serious competition went on the central panel, alongside the gearshift.

▲ The original engines for the Sports were 377-cid V-8s with aluminum heads and hemi combustion chambers fitted with Rochester fuel injection. However, the Nassau cars carried four dual sidedraft 58mm Weber carbs.

▲ Two Grand Sports were later converted into roadsters to compete in Daytona's Continental. Excessive drag of the coupe body, it was feared, would limit top speed. Because of GM management's intervention, the cars never entered that event. Driver George Wintersteen bought this one, and installed a 427-cid V-8.

President Lyndon Johnson signed the Civil Rights Act on July 3. In August, the bodies of three civil rights workers were found buried near Philadelphia, Mississippi. Dr. Martin Luther King, Jr., was awarded the Nobel Peace Prize.

The Beatles arrived in New York in February to appear on the *Ed Sullivan Show*, where they played to a frenzied crowd of fans. New York hosted the first World's Fair since 1939, while the Olympics took place in Tokyo. Leonid Brezhnev ousted Nikita Khrushchev as Soviet premier.

In January, U.S. Surgeon General Luther L. Terry declared smoking to be a health hazard. In November, Lyndon Johnson and his vice-president, Hubert Humphrey, defeated conservative Arizona Senator Barry Goldwater.

•Corvette coupes lose their short-lived split window; new backlight is one-piece

•Corvette hoods no longer hold fake air intakes

•Air-exhaust vents on the pillar are functional, serving as air extractors

•With added body insulation, this year's two-seaters ride smoother and quieter

•Production edges upward, to 22,229 units (13,925 of them convertibles)

•All 1964 American cars have front seatbelts . . . Ford's Mustang debuts at mid-year

▲ Although both body styles had sold equally well in 1963, only 8304 of the 22,229 Sting Rays built this year were coupes. Prices remained the same as before: $4252 for the coupe and $4037 for the roadster (convertible).

▲ After only a single year of production, the Sting Ray coupe's split rear window was gone, replaced by one-piece glass. Visibility was better, of course, but the coupe lost some of its appeal. The fuel filler door gained concentric circles.

▲ Though carrying on with the basic theme set down in 1963, the '64 styling study carried a rather awesome set of headers and side pipes where a pair of simulated fender vents ordinarily sit. This car was later shown at the 1964 World's Fair.

▲ Fake vents on coupe's rear pillars became functional on the left side, helping keep interior air fresh.

▲ Roadsters showed less visible change than coupes. However, new variable-rate springs helped improve the ride.

1964 Selected Colors

Saddle Tan Met.

Riverside Red

Ermine White

Daytona Blue Met.

Silver Blue Met.

Satin Silver Met.

Tuxedo Black

DIMENSIONS

Wheelbase (in.):	98
Overall length (in.):	175.3
Overall height (in.):	49.8
Overall width (in.):	69.6
Track front/rear (in.):	56.3/57
Curb weight (lbs):	3180

ENGINE SPECS

1964	Std.	L75	L76	L84
Type:	ohv V-8	ohv V-8	ohv V-8	ohv V-8
Bore X stroke (in.):	4.00 X 3.25	4.00 X 3.25	4.00 X 3.25	4.00 X 3.25
Displacement (ci):	327	327	327	327
Compression ratio:	10.5:1	10.5:1	11.25:1[1]	11:1[1]
Horsepower @ rpm (bhp):	250 @ 4400	300 @ 5000	365 @ 6200	375 @ 6200
Torque @ rpm (lbs/feet):	350 @ 2800	360 @ 3200	350 @ 4000	350 @ 4400
Fuel Delivery:	1 X 4-bbl.	1 X 4-bbl. (AFB)	1 X 4-bbl. (AFB)	Ramjet Fuel Injection
Transmission:	3- or 4-speed manual, Powerglide	3- or 4-speed manual, Powerglide	3- or 4-speed manual	3- or 4-speed manual

[1] "High-Lift" cam

▲ Rocker panels had fewer ribs, with black paint between each one. Inside, the steering wheel carried simulated walnut trim, and instrument bezels were painted flat black.

▲ The fake hood air intakes from 1963 were deleted this year, but their indents remained. More than 80 percent of 'Vettes had the Positraction option listing for $43.05.

▶ Top V-8 was the $538 fuel-injected version, which added 15 horses. Its 375 bhp could deliver 5.6-second 0-60 times.

▼ Crossed flags continued as Corvette's theme. The sintered-metallic brakes were offered in a near racing package for $629.50.

▶ Zora Arkus-Duntov had a hand in creating this hand-built, rear-engined XP-819 Corvette prototype. A 350-bhp, 327-cid V-8 drove a two-speed automatic transaxle. The car had rack-and-pinion steering and a central backbone chassis.

▲ Cleaner styling and engineering improvements refined the '64 edition of "America's sports car." Extra sound insulation helped quiet the interior.

► Drivetrain choices started with a 250-bhp, 327-cid V-8. This car has the step-up 300-bhp version. The solid-lifter engine got a high-lift, long-duration cam and big carb, to yield 365 bhp.

▼ Wheel covers were simplified with nine slim radial slots. Four-speed gearboxes were now made in GM's Muncie, Indiana, plant; the Borg-Warner T10s were no longer used.

▲ Hidden headlights operated via electric motors that were actually electric window lifts. An emergency hand knob was often used.

President Johnson's State of the Union address called for a "Great Society." In July, he authorized Medicare.

The American role in Vietnam escalated during 1965, from advising to actual combat. By year's end, 154,000 troops were in that country. Anti-war protests were building at home.

The East Coast suffered a week-long power blackout in November. Beatnik poet Allen Ginsberg spoke of "Flower Power" at an anti-war rally, previewing a counterculture theme. Ralph Nader broadsided the auto industry with his book, *Unsafe at Any Speed.*

Black leader Malcolm X was assassinated in February. Dr. Martin Luther King, Jr., led a march from Selma to Montgomery, Alabama, to secure voting rights for blacks. Riots erupted in August in the Watts section of Los Angeles.

• Except for a smoothed hood and addition of open fender louvers, Corvettes show little change

• Nearly all Corvettes are sold with new four-wheel disc brake option

• At mid-year, a 425-bhp, 396-cid Mark IV V-8 engine joins the selection of 327s

• Corvette production rises again, to 23,562

• Mako Shark II show car appears

• U.S. car production sets record at 9,335,277 units; Chevrolet produces more than 3 million vehicles.

▲ Bodily changes for the '65 Sting Ray included a fresh black-out horizontal grille and even-cleaner rocker panel moldings. More obvious yet were the triple vertical front fender slots, replacing the twin horizontal ones from '64. The hood was now smooth-surfaced, with indentations deleted.

▲ All told, styling revisions were modest. Mechanically, the big news was the arrival of optional four-wheel disc brakes. Only 316 cars, in fact, had drum binders, which were a $64.50 credit option. The all-disc system with vented rotors for cooling was accompanied by special wheel covers.

▲ The specially bulged hood on this Sting Ray coupe, which is being painted in the St. Louis plant, indicates that a big-block (396-cid) V-8 engine will go underneath. In addition to the aggressive hood shape, Corvettes with the big engine got a special rear sway bar, super-heavy-duty clutch, and larger radiator and fan.

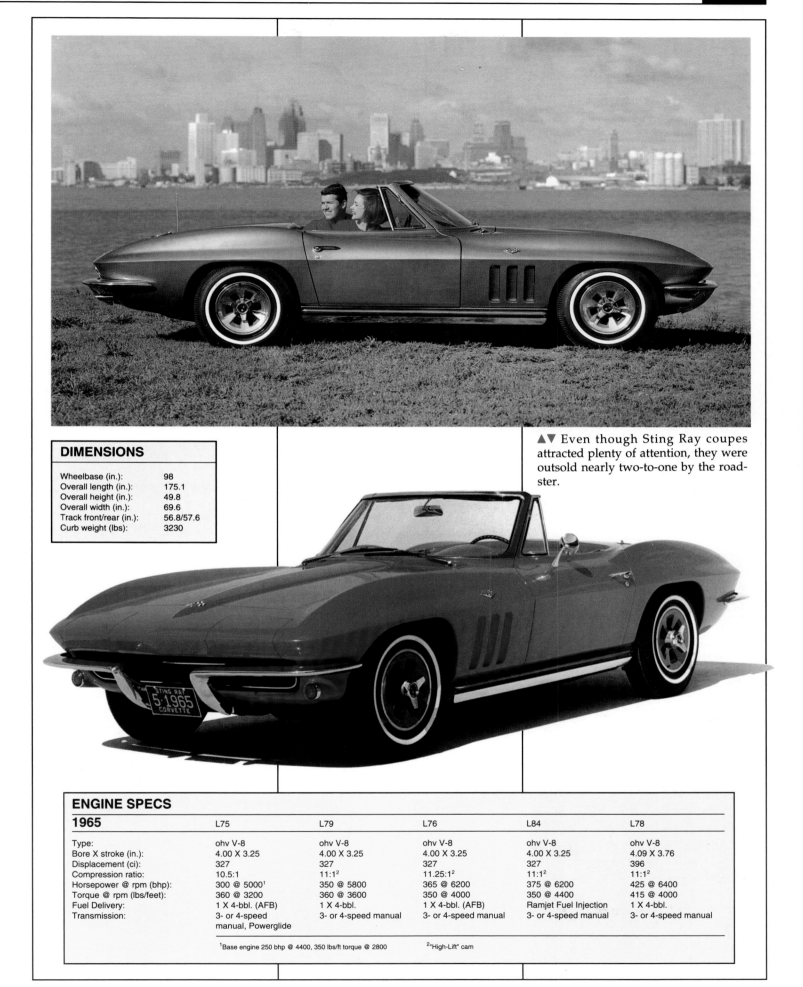

▲▼ Even though Sting Ray coupes attracted plenty of attention, they were outsold nearly two-to-one by the roadster.

DIMENSIONS

Wheelbase (in.):	98
Overall length (in.):	175.1
Overall height (in.):	49.8
Overall width (in.):	69.6
Track front/rear (in.):	56.8/57.6
Curb weight (lbs):	3230

ENGINE SPECS

1965	L75	L79	L76	L84	L78
Type:	ohv V-8	ohv V-8	ohv V-8	ohv V-8	ohv V-8
Bore X stroke (in.):	4.00 X 3.25	4.00 X 3.25	4.00 X 3.25	4.00 X 3.25	4.09 X 3.76
Displacement (ci):	327	327	327	327	396
Compression ratio:	10.5:1	11:1[2]	11.25:1[2]	11:1[2]	11:1[2]
Horsepower @ rpm (bhp):	300 @ 5000[1]	350 @ 5800	365 @ 6200	375 @ 6200	425 @ 6400
Torque @ rpm (lbs/feet):	360 @ 3200	360 @ 3600	350 @ 4000	350 @ 4400	415 @ 4000
Fuel Delivery:	1 X 4-bbl. (AFB)	1 X 4-bbl.	1 X 4-bbl. (AFB)	Ramjet Fuel Injection	1 X 4-bbl.
Transmission:	3- or 4-speed manual, Powerglide	3- or 4-speed manual	3- or 4-speed manual	3- or 4-speed manual	3- or 4-speed manual

[1]Base engine 250 bhp @ 4400, 350 lbs/ft torque @ 2800   [2]"High-Lift" cam

▲ Will it be a cozy Sting Ray fastback coupe or a fun-in-the-sun roadster? Talk about tough decisions! Corvette production rose to 23,562 this year, with the roadster (convertible) accounting for 15,376 units and coupes only 8186. Prices edged up to $4106 for the roadster and $4321 for the coupe. This was the final year for a fuel-injected engine.

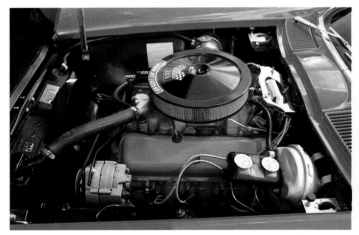

▲ Arriving at mid-year was a 396-cid Turbo Jet V-8—part of the Mark IV "porcupine" engine family (so nicknamed for the shape of its valvegear). This solid-lifter edition with 11.0:1 compression whipped out a thundering 425 horsepower.

▲ Base engine for 1965 was again the 327-cid V-8, offered with four ratings in carbureted form, to deliver 250 to 365 horsepower. Fuel injection, identified by front fender badges, remained available and offered 375 horses.

▲ Top dog in 1965 was the mid-year, 425-bhp Turbo-Jet V-8. This was the first time since fuel injection had been offered, that a carbed engine yielded more horsepower than the top fuelie.

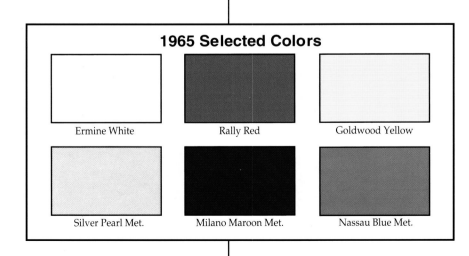

1965 Selected Colors

Ermine White	Rally Red	Goldwood Yellow
Silver Pearl Met.	Milano Maroon Met.	Nassau Blue Met.

▲ Bill Mitchell stands in beside the Mako Shark II. Built on a Sting Ray chassis, the car toured auto shows to test public reaction regarding the new body style. This second example was built as a running prototype.

▲ Inside, the Mako Shark II differed dramatically from the Sting Ray's interior. A huge console held rocker switches and thumbwheels. Note the strange shape of the pedals. Mako II was one of Chevy's most famous show cars.

▶ Tough-looking side-mounted exhaust pipes were optional with the new 396-cid "porcupine" V-8, a logical choice to complement its 425-bhp rating. Though in short supply, the big-block was a hot performer for those lucky enough to get one. Even with modest 3.70:1 gearing, it could run the quarter-mile in just over 14 seconds, hitting 102 mph or more, and accelerate to 60 mph in 5.7 seconds. A 375-bhp fuelie comes in just behind at 14.4 and 99 mph for the quarter and 6.3 seconds in the 0-60 dash.

▲ Carrying on the styling theme of the Mako I, the Mako Shark II wore a lower snout and shorter tail. Pictured above is the non-running show car of 1965.

▲ Practical-minded enthusiasts could pay an extra $236.75 and get a removable hardtop for the roadster. Open Corvettes gained in popularity, with volume up 10 percent over 1964.

▲ Gas filler doors got a new emblem this year, but little else changed in back for '65. Inside, new seats had molded back panels, and carpeting was now molded.

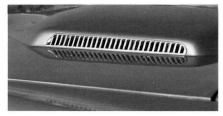

▲ Fans and rivals in '65 scanned Corvette hoods for telltale signs of big-block power. This subtly trimmed bulge was all they needed to see.

▶ The 396-cid V-8's block and head were all-new. Under Corvette hoods, it used an oversize sump and bigger carburetor, with dual-snorkel air cleaner.

▲ The '65 'Vette's standard 4-wheel disc brakes were patterned after the Girling design used on the Grand Sport race cars.

◄ Corvette's twin-cove dash was well developed by this time. A full array of easy-to-read round gauges sat ahead of the driver, with a long, easy-to-grasp gearshift lever close at hand.

▼ The '65's trio of large fender vent openings is evident in this view from the rear. Sting Rays had a down-to-business look, with minimal adornment.

1966

Search-and-destroy missions in the Mekong Delta intensified the American presence in South Vietnam.

Race riots erupted in Chicago and Atlanta in summer, as the "Black Power" movement gained momentum. In the Miranda case, the U.S. Supreme Court ruled that criminal suspects must be informed of their rights. The National Traffic and Motor Vehicle Safety Act was enacted, and the Department of Transportation established.

In November, Ronald Reagan was elected governor of California. In China, the Cultural Revolution was underway.

Masters and Johnson issued their authoritative study of sexuality, *Human Sexual Response*, as miniskirts took hold of the fashion world.

•Corvette sales set another record, with 27,720 built, more than one-third coupes

•Eggcrate inserts replace the horizontal grille bars, ribbed rocker moldings are installed, and coupes lose their roof vents

•Telltale sign of a new Turbo-Jet 427-cid V-8 is the "power bulge" hood; up to 425 bhp is available

•With the hottest engine, a 'Vette can rip to 60 mph in as little as 4.8 seconds

•Options include side-mounted exhaust system

•Fuel injection for the 327 V-8 is dropped this year

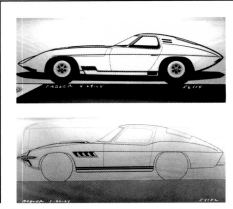

▲ These large-scale renderings of potential Corvette restyles were created between March and July of 1964. Each continues the basic Sting Ray theme, but details differ. Note the steeply-sloped windshield, with lack of evident pillar, at upper left.

▲ GM stylists were pondering updates for '66 in April 1964. This clay wore a split-grille front end and shallow rear window. Note the two taillight treatments.

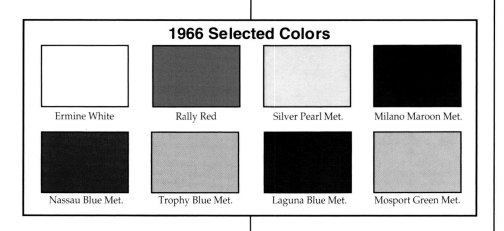

1966 Selected Colors

Ermine White	Rally Red	Silver Pearl Met.	Milano Maroon Met.
Nassau Blue Met.	Trophy Blue Met.	Laguna Blue Met.	Mosport Green Met.

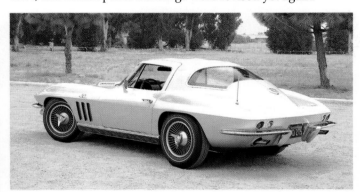

▲ Because the '66 Sting Ray was expected to be the last of its generation, it changed only slightly. The eggcrate grille was new, and rocker panel moldings were revised yet again.

▲ The most notable change was the deletion of vents on coupe C-pillars. Fender badges and hood bulge revealed a new "427 Turbo Jet" V-8, capable of 0-60 mph in under five seconds.

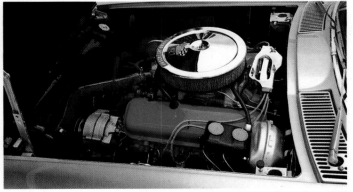

▲ Nothing in this year's interior was unfamiliar to Sting Ray fans. Deep-dish steering wheels had triple metal spokes and the option of a teakwood rim.

▲ Under some Sting Ray hoods, the 396 V-8 was bored to 427 cid, cranking out 390 or (as shown here) 425 horsepower. Fuel injection had now been dropped.

▲ By production time, the inefficient pillar-mounted air vents shown on this prototype were gone. The '66 was expected to be the final Sting Ray, but the design would last one more year.

▲ Powertrain choices dropped in number. Base engine was now a 300-horsepower edition of the 327 V-8, while $105 bought the step-up L79 with 350 horsepower.

▶ More than 89 percent of Corvettes had a $184 four-speed manual gearbox, in either close- or wide-ratio. Only two percent kept the standard three-speed.

▲ The sharply bulged fenders of the Sting Ray stand out when viewed from the rear, as on this roadster with a detachable hardtop. The convertible/roadster now listed at $4084, and production rose to 17,762 units. Coupes started at $4295 and 9958 were built (1772 more than '65), bringing the total to an impressive 27,720.

ENGINE SPECS

1966	L75	L79	L36	L72
Type:	ohv V-8	ohv V-8	ohv V-8	ohv V-8
Bore X stroke (in.):	4.00 X 3.25	4.00 X 3.25	4.25 X 3.76	4.25 X 3.76
Displacement (ci):	327	327	427	427
Compression ratio:	10.5:1	11:1[1]	10.25:1[1]	10.25:1[1]
Horsepower @ rpm (bhp):	300 @ 5000	350 @ 5800	390 @ 5400	425 @ 5600
Torque @ rpm (lbs/feet):	360 @ 3200	360 @ 3600	460 @ 3600	460 @ 4000
Fuel Delivery:	1 X 4-bbl.	1 X 4-bbl.	1 X 4-bbl.	1 X 4-bbl.
Transmission:	3- or 4-speed manual, Powerglide	3- or 4-speed manual	3- or 4-speed manual	3- or 4-speed manual

[1] "High-Lift" cam

▲ Side exhaust notwithstanding, spotters knew this roadster had big-block power. Nothing could beat a 427 'Vette except a Cobra, which was a stark semi-competition machine, not a sport tourer.

◄ ▲ Initially assessed at 450 horsepower, the top 427 V-8 was later downrated to 425 bhp, with 460 lbs/ft of torque.

▲ Even without the hottest engine and performance options, an open or closed Sting Ray had plenty of pizzazz. Only one in five came with power steering, which added $94.80.

▲ Corvettes could be equipped for touring or performance. Air conditioning cost $413, and leather seats $79. Both goldwall nylon and whitewall rayon tires were available.

1967

For the first time, American troops shelled targets inside North Vietnam. Minnesota Senator Eugene McCarthy announced that he would challenge fellow Democrat Lyndon Johnson, and run for president on an anti-war platform. Anti-war protests peaked with a march on the Pentagon in October.

Thurgood Marshall became the first black appointed to the U.S. Supreme Court, not long after the nation's worst racial riot broke out in Detroit. Muhammad Ali (formerly Cassius Clay) was stripped of his boxing title for resisting the draft.

A Six-Day War erupted in the Middle East—the third Arab-Israeli conflict.

San Francisco's Haight-Ashbury district had become a mecca for hippie "flower children," who celebrated a "Summer of Love."

• Changes include a single oblong backup light, revised front fender louvers, and bolt-on aluminum wheels

• Optional this year: a black vinyl covering for the roadster's removable hardtop

• Engine selection is unchanged; with triple carburetors, the 427 V-8 develops 435 bhp

• Dave Morgan and Don Yenko place 10th overall and first in GT at the Sebring race

• GM produces its 100-millionth vehicle

▲ Not much up front separated the 1967 Sting Ray from its '66 predecessor. This would be its final season before making way for the "Shark."

▲ Notice the backup light—mounted above the license plate—a feature that separates the '67 from other Sting Rays.

▲ A restyled, striped hood scoop suggested the presence of a big-block engine, with 390, 400 or 435 horsepower. For all-out "go," Chevrolet offered the ultimate: a wild L89 option, rated 425 bhp but really running some 560 horsepower on 12.5:1 compression with big-gulp Holley carburetion. Only 20 were made, adding $1500 to the price tag.

1967 Selected Colors

Ermine White	Silver Pearl Met.	Rally Red	Sunfire Yellow
Elkhart Blue Met.	Lynndale Blue Met.	Goodwood Green Met.	Marlboro Maroon Met.

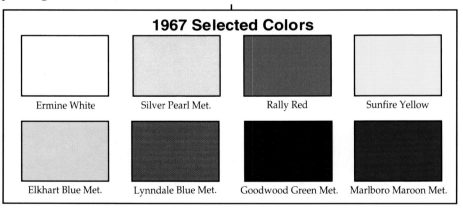

▲ Front fenders got another touchup, now sporting five angled vent holes on each side instead of three. Flat-black and aluminum rocker panels brought a lower, less chunky look. Rally wheels replaced the ornate, old-fashioned wheel covers.

▲ The next generation was taking shape, as this early 1965 rendering (intended for a '67 restyle) indicates. Prominent details included a low, pointed nose, as on the Mako Shark II show car, and bulges over each wheel. This roofline would not see actual production.

DIMENSIONS

Wheelbase (in.):	98
Overall length (in.):	175.1
Overall height (in.):	49.8
Overall width (in.):	69.6
Track front/rear (in.):	56.8/57.6
Curb weight (lbs):	3360

▼ ▶ With 390 horsepower, the L36 edition of the 427-cid V-8 cost $200.15 extra. A triple-carb L68 variant offered 10 more horses for $305. Both had 10.25:1 compression, unlike the 11.0:1 squeeze employed by the 435-bhp engine with its solid lifters and transistor ignition.

▶ Sting Ray interiors again featured the twin-cowl theme, but upholstery patterns changed slightly. The parking brake was relocated between the two seats. New safety features included a dual-circuit brake system (with warning light), energy-absorbing steering column and instrument panel, and provisions for shoulder harnesses.

▼ Slotted six-inch Rally wheels came with chrome beauty rings. Their lug nuts hid behind small chrome hubcaps.

▲ Hood striping added some snarl to the Corvette's image. A side-mounted exhaust added $131.65 to the sport coupe's $4353 base price. Aluminum wheels (shown) cost $263.30.

▲ With headlights open or shut, the '67 was considered the cleanest-looking Corvette of the Sting Ray generation. Hood scoop and "427" designation reveal a potent big-block.

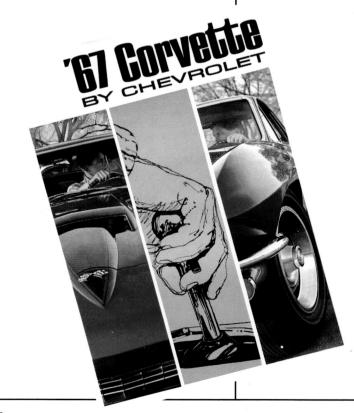

▲ The hottest performer of the 427-cid V-8 trio got a boost to 435 bhp and cost $437. Aluminum cylinder heads added $368.

◀ For yet another season, Chevrolet offered true sports-car fans an American-built choice with the Sting Ray. Before long, the focus on performance would fall victim to changing times.

▲ Standard blackwall tires conveyed a stark, dangerous look—especially with side exhaust lurking below the door.

▲ A 327-cid V-8 with 350 horsepower couldn't match the 427, but was no slouch. The base engine developed 300 horses.

ENGINE SPECS

1967	L79	L36	L68	L71	L88
Type:	ohv V-8	ohv V-8	ohv V-8	ohv V-8	ohv V-8, aluminum heads
Bore X stroke (in.):	4.00 X 3.25	4.25 X 3.76	4.25 X 3.76	4.25 X 3.76	4.25 X 3.76
Displacement (ci):	327	427	427	427	427
Compression ratio:	11.0:1[1]	10.25:12[1]	10.25:1[1]	10.25:1[1]	12.5:1[1]
Horsepower @ rpm (bhp):	350 @ 5800[2]	390 @ 5400	400 @ 5400	435 @ 5800	430 @ 5200
Torque @ rpm (lbs/feet):	360 @ 3600	460 @ 3600	460 @ 3600	460 @ 4000	450 @ 4400
Fuel Delivery:	1 X 4-bbl.	1 X 4-bbl.	3 X 2-bbl.	3 X 2-bbl.	1 X 4-bbl. (850 cfm)
Transmission:	3- or 4-speed manual	3- or 4-speed manual	3- or 4-speed manual	3- or 4-speed manual	3- or 4-speed manual

[1]"High-Lift" cam   [2]Base L48 engine 300 bhp @ 5000, 360 lbs/ft torque @ 3200, 10.5:1 compression

▲ With the base 300-bhp powerplant, a Corvette with stick shift could hit 60 mph in 7.8 seconds and run the quarter-mile in 16. Top speed was 121 mph. These are impressive numbers even today.

▲ Corvette represented the ultimate in performance and sex appeal to an entire generation of young Americans. Today, Sting Rays rank among the most prized 'Vettes of all.

▲ For the first time, two hardtops were available for the convertible 'Vette—the body color top and a black vinyl top.

▲ A "427" badge could mean any of three horsepower ratings.

▶ The sizzler of the lot was the L71 option, with triple carburetion and 435 eager horses waiting to be unleashed.

▼ Final Sting Rays tolled the end of an exciting era, soon to be subdued by new attitudes and government regulations.

▲ Created for competition, the Le Mans Corvette of Bob Bondurant and Dick Guldstrand ran a strong first in its class at that marathon. However, its engine failed near the end of the race.

▲ Under the hood of this Le Mans Corvette lies a rare L88 engine, whose air cleaner sealed against the hood.

▲ In addition to Le Mans competition, a 'Vette driven by Bob Hirsch hit a record 192.879 mph at the Bonneville Salt Flats.

▲ Even with a minimum of extra equipment and standard Rally wheels, a Sting Ray fastback was hard to resist in '67.

▲ Production slumped this year to 14,436 roadsters and 8504 coupes. A coupe sold for $4353, the roadster for $4141.

In January, the North Vietnamese launched a huge "Tet Offensive," attacking major cities in the south. Two months later, Lyndon Johnson announced that he would not seek a second term. Meanwhile, Eugene McCarthy had scored a surprise victory in the New Hampshire Democratic primary.

Americans were shocked by two assassinations: Dr. Martin Luther King, Jr., in April and, two months later, presidential candidate Robert Kennedy.

Marred by anguished protests and venomous police response at the convention in Chicago, a severely split Democratic Party nominated Hubert Humphrey for president. He lost to Richard Nixon.

Tom Wolfe published *The Electric Kool-Aid Acid Test*, a caustic observation of the counterculture.

• Bulged fenders and a tunneled roofline mark the radically restyled Corvette, dubbed the "Shark"

• Styling retains the ground-hugging snout of the Mako Shark II show car, but adds a Kamm-style rear deck

• Wind-tunnel testing produces several changes prior to production

• Larger fender louvers are needed to improve cooling

• Coupe roof panels and rear glass are removable, giving an open air feel

• Corvette production sets new record

▲ Styling of the Mako Shark II gave it a born-runner look, symbolized by the shark insignia. Bill Mitchell wanted the next 'Vette to adopt much of the Mako look.

▲ While the first Mako II toured shows, this running prototype was being prepared. At the rear, round taillamps carried over.

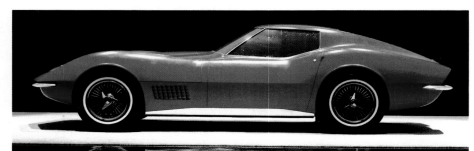

▲ Except for its roof, this fastback clay gives a fair estimate of the new profile. Closer inspection reveals differences in front fender vents and door handles.

▲ Compared to the production "Shark," the front end of this early clay shows variances in the grille.

▲ Production Corvettes differed from this clay model in roof/window style and the addition of a ducktail spoiler.

◀ Though rather fanciful in tone, this rendering of a racing roadster isn't far removed from the profile of the final '68 Corvette. Note the long, low nose, aimed toward the ground. GM design chief Bill Mitchell wanted a different look, so he encouraged his stylists to come up with plenty of fresh ideas, using Mako II as a foundation.

▲ This trimmed clay from November 1965 looks near production, except for hood bulge and grille.

▲ This December 1965 clay lacks the chrome bumpers and grille cutout of its eventual production successor.

▲ Six round taillights on this trimmed clay of November 1965 turned out to be two more than the production Corvette. The "flying buttress" roofline also would be revised.

▲ A clay model from December 1965 shows how close the stylists had finally come to settling on a roofline. Rectangular taillights defied Corvette tradition, and were wisely skipped.

▲ Many basic elements were set by the time of this early clay model, but refinements had yet to be developed. Final cars would have thumb-operated door handles with chrome grips.

▲ Vents ahead of front wheels on November 1965 clay were destined to be replaced by side marker lights. Those behind the wheels would change shape, becoming vertical "gills."

▲ GM design chief Bill Mitchell poses with the Mako Shark II and a production coupe. The sales catalog called Corvette "the true sports car from Chevrolet. . . . made for people who feel that the best part of living is driving."

▶ A huge round speedo and tach starred in a new dash with fresh-air inlets. Stale air exited through deck vents. Bucket seats were narrower; seatbacks steeper. Some observers faulted the center planel location of secondary gauges.

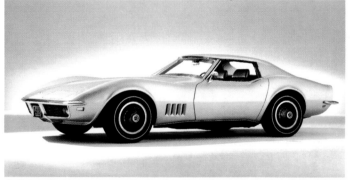

▲ Four large, nearly vertical vents decorated front fenders. Horizontal door pulls sat at the upper corners.

▼ The non-running Astro 'Vette show car's narrow nose held tiny air slots. Low air drag was the theme.

▲ Viewed from the side, the coupe looked like a fastback, but the rear window was almost vertical and could be removed.

1968 Selected Colors

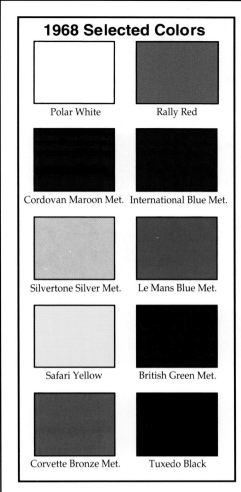

Polar White

Rally Red

Cordovan Maroon Met.

International Blue Met.

Silvertone Silver Met.

Le Mans Blue Met.

Safari Yellow

British Green Met.

Corvette Bronze Met.

Tuxedo Black

DIMENSIONS

Wheelbase (in.):	98
Overall length (in.):	182.1
Overall height (in.):	47.8
Overall width (in.):	69.6
Track front/rear (in.):	58.3/59
Curb weight (lbs):	3425

▲ Styling was surely distinctive—even exotic, compared to most road cars. To sports car purists, it was controversial, if not downright excessive. *Road & Track* even labeled it a "psychedelic car." Testers faulted the low roofline, long front end, cramped interior, skimpy cargo hold, and the overall poor fit/finish.

▲ Rear-end styling retained the familiar four taillights. Chevrolet explained that a "long, low profile with blunt styling brings up the rear." Convertibles had a rear-hinged top cover, and an optional vinyl roof now held a glass window.

▲ A display cutaway of the '68 Corvette gave prospective customers a close and detailed look at its engine, cockpit, and luggage area. A raised platform held the car, so viewers could see underneath. Production set a record at 28,566.

ENGINE SPECS

1968	L79	L36	L68	L71	L88
Type:	ohv V-8	ohv V-8	ohv V-8	ohv V-8	ohv V-8, aluminum heads
Bore X stroke (in.):	4.00 X 3.25	4.25 X 3.76	4.25 X 3.76	4.25 X 3.76	4.25 X 3.76
Displacement (ci):	327	427	427	427	427
Compression ratio:	11:1[1]	10.25:1[1]	10.25:1[1]	11.0:1[1]	12.5:1[1]
Horsepower @ rpm (bhp):	350 @ 5800[2]	390 @ 5400	400 @ 5400	435 @ 5800	430 @ 5200
Torque @ rpm (lbs/feet):	360 @ 3600	460 @ 3600	460 @ 3600	460 @ 4000	450 @ 4400
Fuel Delivery:	1 X 4-bbl.	1 X 4-bbl.	3 X 2-bbl.	3 X 2-bbl.	1. X 4-bbl. (850 cfm)
Transmission:	4-speed manual	4-speed manual, Turbo Hydra-Matic	4-speed manual, Turbo Hydra-Matic	4-speed manual	4-speed manual

[1]Duntov "High-Lift" cam   [2]Base L48 engine 300 bhp @ 5000, 360 lbs/ft torque @ 3400, 10.0:1 compression

▶ A bulged hood announced the presence of a 427 V-8. Controversial Hide-A-Way wiper/washers hid under a power, vacuum-operated panel.

▼ Vent wings were gone, so "Astro Ventilation" passed air through with windows shut, arriving via ventiports.

▲ Except for rocker panel moldings, '68 Corvette bodysides were devoid of chrome trim. Lack of vent windows made the convertible's lines a tad cleaner.

▶ This year's Turbo Jet 427-cid V-8 came in three standard ratings: 390, 400, and 435 bhp. The hottest two used triple carburetion instead of a four-barrel.

▲ Headlights worked by vacuum. Poor airflow up front made engine cooling a problem.

▲ Engine choices started with the 327-cid V-8, at 300 or 350 bhp. Base gearbox was still a three-speed manual, but close- and wide-ratio four-speeds drew more interest. GM's new three-speed Turbo Hydra-Matic replaced Powerglide as an option.

▲ Even in the early plans for Sting Ray's successor a Targa roof was included. To reduce body flex, a two-pane T-top took its place.

▶ Coupe roofs held "flying buttress" sail panels, flanking an upright rear window.

▼ If 435 horses wouldn't do, racers could order the rare L88 edition of the 427 V-8. Nominally 430 bhp, it yielded up to 560 bhp.

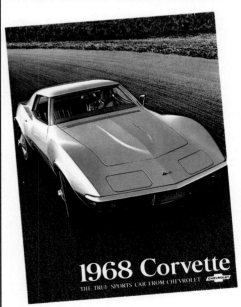

▲ Sales literature touted such features as Hide-A-Way wipers and "functional louvers [to] help keep the horses cool."

◀ At the track, competition was stiff with Ford's GT enduro racers and sponsors wasted no time in switching to the new Corvette's more aerodynamic body.

1969

The first American combat unit left Vietnam in July, as part of Richard Nixon's plan to turn fighting over to the South Vietnamese. Late in the year, Americans learned of the My Lai massacre of 1968, in which U.S. troops killed hundreds of civilians.

Warren E. Burger was confirmed as Chief Justice of the Supreme Court. White House press secretary Ron Ziegler first used the term "photo opportunity." Vice-President Spiro Agnew, angered by anti-war and anti-establishment ideas, dubbed journalists "nattering nabobs of negativism."

American astronauts Neil Armstrong and Edwin Aldrin walked on the moon in July, proclaiming that "The eagle has landed."

Soon to become legendary, a weekend music festival near Woodstock, New York, drew some 400,000 avid fans. *Easy Rider* and *Midnight Cowboy* lured moviegoers.

• Stingray name returns to Corvettes, which change little this year

• Pushbutton door openers are dropped

• For the first time, the coupe outsells its convertible mate

• Standard Corvette engine is now a 350-cid V-8, but four 427s also are available

• Wider-rim wheels improve handling, while a stiffer frame eliminates shake

• Production sets yet another record, at 38,762 Corvettes

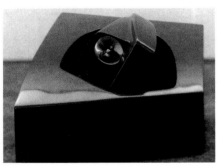

▲ One design consideration for the fifth generation was creating better headlights and refining the lights' pop-up operation. This design had small "projection" lights mounted on a rotating platform. But cost considerations and government regulations forced standard lights on pop-up mounts.

▶ The '69 improved in fit and finish. A coupe listed at $4781, the ragtop at $4438, with standard four-wheel disc brakes and new headlight washers. Output hit 38,762.

1969 Selected Colors

| Can-Am White | Le Mans Blue Met. | Fathom Green Met. | Cortez Silver Met. |
| Daytona Yellow | Monza Red | Riverside Gold Met. | Burgundy Met. |

▲ Most obvious of the changes for 1969 was the return of the Stingray name—now spelled as one word—decorating front fenders. Because the '68 had changed so much, no one expected much alteration this year, but Chevrolet designers were always tinkering with the details. One big option was side-mount exhaust systems. Front-fender louver trim was a popular dress-up option at $21.10.

DIMENSIONS

Wheelbase (in.):	98
Overall length (in.):	182.5
Overall height (in.):	47.9
Overall width (in.):	69.0
Track front/rear (in.):	58.7/59.4
Curb weight (lbs):	3260

ENGINE SPECS

1969	L46	L36	L68	L71	L88
Type:	ohv V-8	ohv V-8	ohv V-8	ohv V-8	ohv V-8, aluminum heads
Bore X stroke (in.):	4.00 X 3.48	4.25 X 3.76	4.25 X 3.76	4.25 X 3.76	4.25 X 3.76
Displacement (ci):	350	427	427	427	427
Compression ratio:	11.0:1[1]	10.25:1[1]	10.25:1[1]	11.0:1[1]	12.5:1[1]
Horsepower @ rpm (bhp):	350 @ 5600[2]	390 @ 5400	400 @ 5400	435 @ 5800	430 @ 5200
Torque @ rpm (lbs/feet):	380 @ 3600	460 @ 3600	460 @ 3600	460 @ 4000	450 @ 4400
Fuel Delivery:	1 X 4-bbl.	1 X 4-bbl.	3 X 2-bbl.	3 X 2-bbl.	1 X 4-bbl. (850 cfm)
Transmission:	4-speed manual, Turbo Hydra-Matic	4-speed manual, Turbo Hydra-Matic	4-speed manual, Turbo Hydra-Matic	4-speed manual, Turbo Hydra-Matic	4-speed manual, Turbo Hydra-Matic

[1]"High-Lift " cam   [2]Base L48 engine 300 bhp @ 4800, 380 lbs/ft torque @ 3200, 10.25:1 compression

▲ An L88 'Vette looks mighty mean in black. Like other '69s, it rode a stiffer frame and wider (eight-inch) wheels to better handle all that power.

▶ Laughingly underrated at 430 bhp, the brutish L88 engine, wearing aluminum heads, cost a whopping $1032.

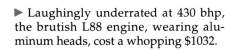

▲ Gulping air through a scoop at the base of the windshield, an L88 was all strength and pure speed.

  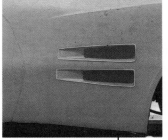 

▲ Even relatively minor design aspects, such as fender vents, underwent serious scrutiny year after year, searching for the perfect shape, size, and number.

◄ A coupe's T-top and removable rear window offered the breezy fun of a convertible, but far better weather and theft protection. The retooled door panels expanded interior width an inch, and the steering wheel diameter was cut by an inch. A wise buyer might have invested $42.15 extra for custom shoulder belts and $11.60 for a speed warning. Side exhaust was optional. For the first time, coupes outsold convertibles, 22,154 to 16,632. Backup lights, previously mounted separately under bumpers, moved into inboard taillights.

▼ Only an expert can tell a 1969 'Vette from a '68 at a glance. Aside from the Stingray badge above fender louvers, chromed door handles with spring-loaded covers were new—and easier to use.

▲ Created in 1969, the Mulsanne show car is seen here with 1975 front and rear facias. Though painted many colors, this car sported the original silver. In addition to its side pipes and special wheels, this car carried high-mounted, side-view mirrors; a periscope-type rear-view mirror; and exposed headlights. The Mulsanne was not only a show car, but also served as the pace car for the Can-Am races—its roof section can be completely removed, allowing the flagman to stand straight up.

1970

After a highly-publicized trial, five of the "Chicago Seven" were found guilty of crossing state lines with intent to cause a riot during demonstrations at the 1968 Democratic convention.

The shooting of four Kent State University students in May by National Guardsmen helped galvanize anti-war dissent. And, "Earth Day" on April 22 brought environmentalism to public consciousness. In April, President Nixon announced that American forces had entered Cambodia. Addressing the nation in November, Nixon referred to the "silent majority."

Two top rock stars, Jimi Hendrix and Janis Joplin, died of drug-related causes. A Boeing 747 flew for the first time this year, and the Concorde hit Mach 2.

- Big-block V-8 grows bigger yet, enlarged to 454 cid with an output of 390 horsepower

- 350-cid V-8 remains available, in three ratings

- Minor changes include an eggcrate pattern in grille and larger parking lights

- Corvette's base price shoots past $5000; volume dips to only 17,316 in a weak year for the industry

- Coupes lead convertibles in sales by about five-to-three

- Chevrolet builds its 70-millionth vehicle

- Japanese challenge grows as imports total 14.6 percent of 1970 car sales

People have the idea you can tell what cars of the future will be like by looking at Chevrolet's Corvette.

They're right.

'70 Corvette

▲ Chevy boasted that the Corvette carried the future. A strike delayed the debut of the '70s, cutting output to 17,316.

▲ Freshening included a revision in fender-vent style. New, flared rear portions of wheelwells helped ease stone chip problems.

▲ An eggcrate pattern appeared on both the grille and the newly chrome-trimmed front-fender vents. Larger parking lights with parabolic reflectors went into outboard corners of the grille. Stainless steel sill moldings also were new.

▲ Bill Mitchell's mildly customized Aero Coupe blended a '69 Corvette with 1970-style crosshatch grille and vents. Other changes: a modest spoiler, one-piece roof, side exhaust, and taller windshield.

▲ Rectangular exhaust trumpets helped give the rear end a more aggressive look. Chevy's 350-cid V-8 came in three ratings. The big-block grew to 454-cid size, with 390 bhp. A 460-bhp LS7 edition was promised, but never became a reality.

ENGINE SPECS

1970	L48	L46	LT1	LS5	LS7
Type:	ohv V-8	ohv V-8	ohv V-8	ohv V-8	ohv V-8
Bore X stroke (in.):	4.00 X 3.48	4.00 X 3.48	4.00 X 3.48	4.25 X 4.00	4.25 X 4.00
Displacement (ci):	350	350	350	454	454
Compression ratio:	10.25:1	11.0:1[1]	11.0:1[1]	10.25:1[1]	11.25:1[1]
Horsepower @ rpm (bhp):	300 @ 4800	350 @ 5600	370 @ 6000	390 @ 4800	460 @ 5600
Torque @ rpm (lbs/feet):	380 @ 3200	380 @ 3600	380 @ 4000	500 @ 3400	490 @ 3000
Fuel Delivery:	1 X 4-bbl.	1 X 4-bbl.	1 X 4-bbl.	1 X 4-bbl.	1 X 4-bbl.
Transmission:	4-speed manual, Turbo Hydra-Matic	4-speed manual	4-speed manual	4-speed manual, Turbo Hydra-Matic	4-speed manual, Turbo Hydra-Matic

[1]"High–Lift " cam

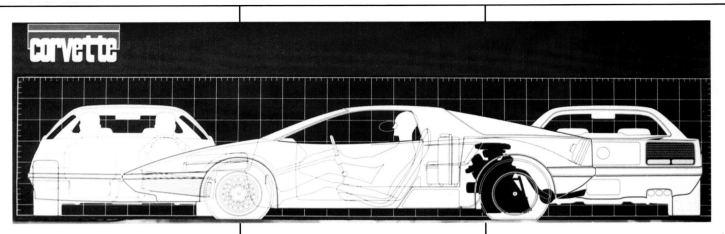

corvette

▲ Chevrolet's focus on the future is evident in these large, see-through renderings of a mid-engined Corvette. The mid-engine configuration nagged at Corvette designers over the years, and resulted in various concept cars. Note the steep slope of the windshield and the position of driver and luggage.

◀ Bodywork for this XP-897 mid-engine coupe with deeply recessed rectangular headlights was performed by Pininfarina, in Italy. Based on a design by GM's Experimental Studio, it rode a modified Porsche 914 frame. The XP-897 featured a two-rotor engine. Notice the differences between right and left sides.

▲ Project XP-882 began on a chassis finished in early 1969. The sharp fastback coupe wore a low, squarish snout with hidden headlights, bulged rear fenders, and sported louvered "boattail" at the back.

▶ Appearing at the 1970 New York Auto Show, the XP-882 had a transverse V-8 engine between the rear wheels. The entire aft body section tilted for engine access.

▲ For the ultimate small-block sizzle, buyers could choose an LT1. Corvette seats were reshaped for more support, headroom, and better trunk access.

▼ A solid-lifter LT1 V-8 with special cam cost $447.50, but delivered 370 bhp and the traditional "rap-rap" exhaust note.

DIMENSIONS

Wheelbase (in.):	98
Overall length (in.):	182.5
Overall height (in.):	47.9
Overall width (in.):	69.0
Track front/rear (in.):	58.7/59.4
Curb weight (lbs):	3720

1970 Selected Colors

Classic White

Marlboro Maroon Met.

Corvette Bronze Met.

Daytona Yellow

Monza Red

Bridgehampton Blue Met.

Mulsanne Blue Met.

Donnybrook Green Met.

1971

A springtime anti-war protest drew nearly 200,000 demonstrators to Washington, D.C. More than 7000 of them were arrested. The *New York Times* published the "Pentagon Papers" in June, detailing U.S. involvement in Vietnam.

President Nixon ended the trade embargo against China. A 90-day total wage/price freeze, initiated in August, was followed by flexible guidelines in Phase II.

The Supreme Court ruled that schoolchildren could be bused for integration. The 26th Amendment gave 18-year-olds the right to vote.

Amtrak rail service began, and Disney World opened in Orlando, Florida. Two astronauts drove the Lunar Rover on the moon's surface.

Andrew Lloyd Webber's rock musical, *Jesus Christ Superstar,* opened in New York. On TV, *All in the Family* debuted.

•Horsepower drops, due to emissions standards

•Corvettes receive revised interiors

•Base engine is 270-bhp, 350-cid V-8; optional, a 330-bhp, solid-lifter LT1

•Hydraulic- and solid-lifter versions of 454 big-block offered: 365 or 425 bhp

•High-dome hood indicates high-potency engine

•Rare ZR1 and ZR2 racing packages offered

•Output rises to 14,680 coupes and 7121 roadsters

▲ Sales brochures encouraged Corvette shoppers to "buy an image. . . . A car that looks all hood and wheels. A car that's eager for the open road . . . a pacesetter."

▲ Due in part to a short 1970 model year, '71s barely changed in appearance. Engineers were scampering to meet federal emissions and safety rules, so the base small-block (L48) V-8 ran on 8.5:1 compression ratio and output dropped to 270 bhp.

▲ All four engines could run on no-lead or low-lead fuel. The crosshatch-pattern fender vents and grilles continued as a styling theme. A choice of 10 colors included "firemist" War Bonnet Yellow.

◄ Interiors got a freshening for 1971. Standard vinyl upholstery came in five colors. The Custom Interior Trim included black or dark saddle leather seats, plus wood-look door panels and console. Turbo Hydra-Matic could now be ordered with any engine other than the LT1.

► Hottest Corvettes ran the LS6 option: a 454-cid Turbo-Jet V-8 with aluminum heads, solid lifters, high-performance cam, 9.0:1 compression, large four-barrel carburetor—and 425 horses (at 5600 rpm). Priced at $1221, the engine was prized at the time and no less eagerly coveted today. Wide- and close-ratio four-speed gearboxes were available.

▲ Ultimate small-block was the LT1, a 350-cid V-8 with solid lifters, 9.0:1 compression, and transistor ignition. Tighter emissions rules and the onset of low-octane gas shrunk bhp numbers from 370 to 330 (275 net, per the rating system that would go industry-wide in 1972).

▲ Sharp fender bulges, a curvaceous profile, and big rectangular exhaust outlets helped maintain the Corvette's "no compromises" image. Two performance suspensions were offered to racers: a ZR1 option with the LT1 engine, and a ZR2 for the LS6 big-block. Only eight ZR1 and 12 ZR2 Corvettes were built this year.

1971 Selected Colors

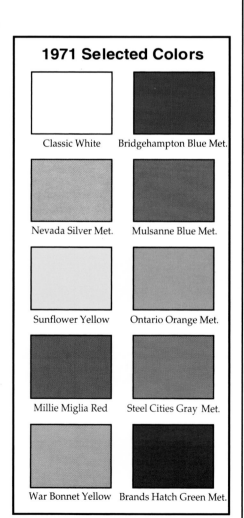

Classic White   Bridgehampton Blue Met.

Nevada Silver Met.   Mulsanne Blue Met.

Sunflower Yellow   Ontario Orange Met.

Millie Miglia Red   Steel Cities Gray Met.

War Bonnet Yellow   Brands Hatch Green Met.

▲ Though evident changes were few, Chevy promoted the "husky-looking larger parking lights" that had debuted earlier. The heavy-duty ZR1/ZR2 options could not be ordered with power windows, power steering, air conditioning, or radio.

ENGINE SPECS

1971	L48	LT1	LS5	LS6
Type:	ohv V-8	ohv V-8	ohv V-8	ohv V-8
Bore X stroke (in.):	4.00 X 3.48	4.00 X 3.48	4.25 X 4.00	4.25 X 4.00
Displacement (ci):	350	350	454	454
Compression ratio:	8.5:1	9.0:1[1]	8.5:1	9.0:1[1]
Horsepower @ rpm (bhp):	270 @ 4800	330 @ 5600	365 @ 4800	425 @ 5600
Torque @ rpm (lbs/feet):	360 @ 3200	360 @ 4000	465 @ 3200	475 @ 4000
Fuel Delivery:	1 X 4-bbl.	1 X 4-bbl.	1 X 4-bbl.	1 X 4-bbl.
Transmission:	4-speed manual, Turbo Hydra-Matic	4-speed manual	4-speed manual, Turbo Hydra-Matic	4-speed manual, Turbo Hydra-Matic

[1]"High-Lift" cam

DIMENSIONS

Wheelbase (in.):	98
Overall length (in.):	182.5
Overall height (in.):	47.9
Overall width (in.):	69.0
Track front/rear (in.):	58.7/59.4
Curb weight (lbs):	3593

▲ Output rose to 7121 convertibles and 14,680 coupes, totaling 21,801. Base price was $5259 for the roadster, $5496 for the coupe. Gas mileage in the 8-16 mpg range wasn't a plus, but in the carefree pre-shortage days, few seemed to worry.

▲ Both hydraulic- and solid-lifter versions of the 454-cid big-block V-8 were offered, with gross ratings of 365 or 425 bhp, respectively.

◀ Big-block engines came with a dual-snorkel air cleaner and oversized oil pan. Also included when ordering a 454: a high-domed hood, thicker front stabilizer bar, rear stabilizer, and large-capacity radiator.

▲ Grille-like fender vents added a racy look to the Stingray. To match its visual impact, 0-60 mph acceleration times ran from 5.3 seconds with an LS6 engine to 7.1 with an L48.

▲ Dashboards still held map pockets, with auxiliary gauges at the central command console. New built-in head restraints on high-back contour bucket seats were standard on coupes.

Once a top "cold warrior," President Nixon visited Red China in February, and Moscow in May. Nixon was re-elected in a landslide, besting George McGovern and gaining 60.7 percent of the popular vote.

Alabama governor George Wallace was shot while campaigning for president. Five men were arrested for burglarizing Democratic headquarters in Washington's Watergate complex.

For the first time in four years, U.S. planes bombed Hanoi and Haiphong as the Vietnam War continued.

J. Edgar Hoover, who'd headed the FBI since its founding in 1924, died on May 2. The Supreme Court ruled the death penalty unconstitutional.

Volkswagen overtook the Model T Ford as the best-selling model of all time. The DDT pesticide was prohibited.

Ms. magazine began publication, and cigarette ads were banned from radio and TV. Notable films included Francis Ford Coppola's *The Godfather.*

• Like other Chevrolets, Corvettes change little but volume rises to 26,994

• This is final year for front/rear chrome bumpers and removable rear window

• Fiber-optic light monitor dropped

• Engines now rated in lower SAE (net) horsepower/torque

• Choices include 200/255-bhp 350 V-8 or 270-bhp big-block; high-output LS6 gone

▲ Except for diminishing of power and performance numbers due to new emissions tuning, this was largely a standstill year. The Turbo-Fire Special LT1 engine dropped from 275 to 255 hp (net). Note its big hood bulge with white striping.

▲ Corvette convertibles came with a black or white folding top, and a vinyl covering was available on the optional removable hardtop. Because the most potent LS6 version of the big-block V-8 was gone, only three engine choices were offered.

Sports car buyer's guide: 1972 Corvette

▲ Power was dropping, but Chevy's sports car hadn't lost its appeal.

▲ Nineteen seventy-two was the last year for the removable rear window. An anti-theft alarm became standard.

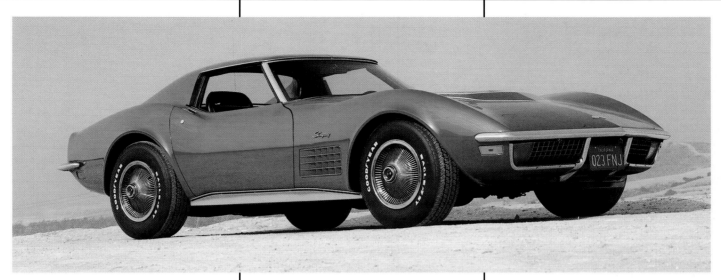

▲ An era was ending as the big-block LS6 departed, leaving only the 365-bhp (270 net) LS5 edition. White-letter tires kept up the image, if not the action.

▲ Standard wheels included bright trim rings and ribbed hubs. A lock at the rear end turned the new audio alarm on/off. Chevrolet described its sound as a "loud, raucous hooting from somewhere under the car." Of this year's ten colors, four were new and three were firemist metallic flake.

▲ The base Turbo-Fire 350 now rated 200 bhp, versus 255 for the LT1 and 270 for the Turbo-Jet 454-cid V-8. Available again, in tiny numbers, was the ZR1 "Special-Purpose" option with the LT1, including special four-speed gearbox. Not recommended for street driving, a ZR1 could not be ordered with power windows, power steering, air conditioning, rear window defroster, wheel covers, or radio.

▲ For its final season in the lineup, the small-block LT1 could be ordered with air conditioning. Tachometers on those cars were redlined at a mild 5600 rpm instead of the usual 6500.

▲ New blue lighting enhanced the speedometer and tach, and all knobs were made of a new soft-feel material.

▲ The era of big, stump-pulling V-8s was fading quickly as the Corvette's most muscular big-block disappeared. Performance would decline further yet, as new emissions rules took effect.

◄ Departing from the lineup after 1971, the 425-bhp LS6 big-block had served Corvette well—and would be fondly remembered. Not that its 365-bhp cousin was a slouch.

▲ Fiber-optic light monitors were dropped, which cleaned up the console. High-rise seats contained built-in head restraints, and coupes had slots for inertia-reel shoulder belts.

ENGINE SPECS

1972 (SAE net bhp ratings)	L48	LT1	LS5
Type:	ohv V-8	ohv V-8	ohv V-8
Bore X stroke (in.):	4.00 X 3.48	4.00 X 3.48	4.25 X 4.00
Displacement (ci):	350	350	454
Compression ratio:	8.5:1	9.0:1[1]	8.5:1
Horsepower @ rpm (bhp):	200 @ 4400	255 @ 5600	270 @ 4000
Torque @ rpm (lbs/feet):	300 @ 2800	280 @ 4000	390 @ 3200
Fuel Delivery:	1 X 4-bbl.	1 X 4-bbl.	1 X 4-bbl.
Transmission:	4-speed manual, Turbo Hydra-Matic	4-speed manual	4-speed manual, Turbo Hydra-Matic

[1] "High-Lift" cam

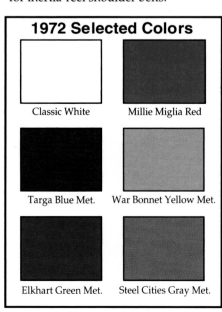

1972 Selected Colors

Classic White	Millie Miglia Red
Targa Blue Met.	War Bonnet Yellow Met.
Elkhart Green Met.	Steel Cities Gray Met.

▲ Unlike many adornments of the '70s, Corvette's fender louvers were functional, venting engine heat. Stainless steel sill moldings and chrome bumpers added decoration.

▲ Interiors were leather-grain vinyl, with leather seats and wood-grain accents optional. Coupes listed for $5533; roadsters, $5296. Output totaled 20,486 coupes and 6508 ragtops.

▲ For years, fans had been hearing rumors of an imminent mid-engine Corvette. Those rumors were fueled once again by the appearance of the sleek silver XP-895 prototype, designed to study prospects for steel/aluminum or all-aluminum unit construction. Note the tapered rear end with recessed taillights.

DIMENSIONS

Wheelbase (in.):	98
Overall length (in.):	182.5
Overall height (in.):	47.9
Overall width (in.):	69.0
Track front/rear (in.):	58.7/59.4
Curb weight (lbs):	3556

▲ Inside, the XP-895 looked only partly familiar with its tall console, simple dash, and twin-spoke steering wheel. Note the form-fitting leather seats.

▲ A 400-cid V-8 with "split" powertrain was mounted amidships in the XP-895, whose body was crafted with assistance from Reynolds Aluminum.

1973

On January 27, after an agreement at the Paris peace accords, the Vietnam War was declared over. The U.S. dollar was devalued.

Watergate conspirators were sentenced to prison. Sam Ervin led the Senate hearings.

Vice-President Spiro Agnew resigned his office, pleading "no contest" to charges of tax evasion. Gerald Ford was sworn in as Agnew's replacement. In November, President Nixon declared: "I'm not a crook."

Sioux Indians engineered a 70-day standoff with federal agents, the "Second Battle of Wounded Knee." In the Roe v. Wade case, the Supreme Court allowed women the right to choose an abortion. Horse-racing fans saw Secretariat take the Triple Crown.

In October, an oil embargo by the Organization of Petroleum Exporting Coun–tries (OPEC) was begun to punish supporters of Israel in the Yom Kippur war.

• Corvettes get first major restyle since 1968

• Federal law mandates 5-mph front bumper, integrated in body-color on Corvettes; rear bumper is usual chrome

• 350-cid V-8 rated 190 horsepower in standard form

• 250-bhp, 350-cid V-8 and 454 big-block (275-bhp) also available; LT1 dropped

• Total production rises again to 30,465 Corvettes, including 24,372 coupes

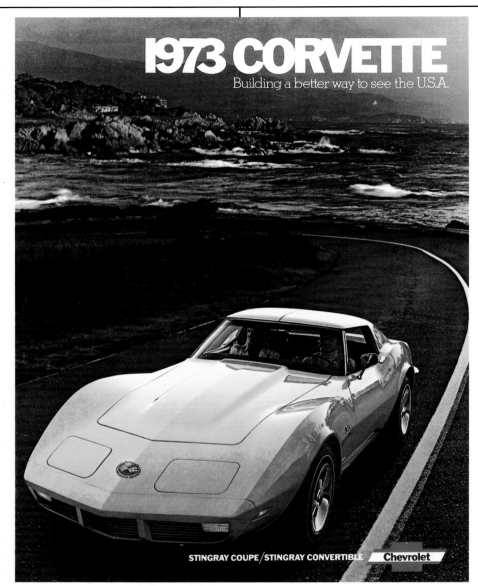

STINGRAY COUPE/STINGRAY CONVERTIBLE   Chevrolet

▲ This year brought the first major restyling of the generation that debuted in '68. The reworked front end featured a body-colored, urethane plastic "soft" nose, designed to bounce back to original shape after a low-speed bump. It was this kind of car, promised the sales brochure, "that brings out the driver in you."

▲ Chevy's response to federally-mandated five-mph bumpers was not only inge-nious, but far more attractive than most such installations. However, chrome bumpers still brought up the rear of America's sports car. New cushioned body mounts and improved acoustical materials created a smoother, quieter ride.

▼ The resilient new bumper added about two inches to overall length and 35 pounds to weight, and sat above a new aluminum grille. Parking/marker lights were highlighted in chrome. Doors contained steel guard rails to deal with side impacts.

▲ Engine outputs dropped again, to 190 bhp for the base 350-cid V-8, 250 bhp for the L82 Turbo-Fire Special (shown), and 275 bhp for the Turbo-Jet 454 (LS4) big-block. Note the air-cleaner lip, which mated with a new domed air-induction hood.

▲ Fixed glass replaced the coupe's removable backlight, increasing trunk space slighty. New GR70 × 15 steel-belted radial-ply tires were claimed to run cooler and give a softer, quieter ride. In addition, they offered longer life, better stability, and improved wet-weather grip.

▲ For the first time since 1956, there was no solid-lifter V-8 in the lineup. All engines, including this L82, ran on regular or no-lead fuel. An exhaust gas recirculation system helped cut emissions, while mufflers were larger and quieter.

▲ Stylish aluminum wheels were a new option, but structural problems forced recall of the first 800 sets.

ENGINE SPECS

1973	L48	L82	LS4
Type:	ohv V-8	ohv V-8	ohv V-8
Bore X stroke (in.):	4.00 X 3.48	4.00 X 3.48	4.25 X 4.00
Displacement (ci):	350	350	454
Compression ratio:	8.5:1	9.0:1	8.25:1
Horsepower @ rpm (bhp):	190 @ 4400	250 @ 5200	275 @ 4400
Torque @ rpm (lbs/feet):	270 @ 2800	285 @ 4000	395 @ 2800
Fuel Delivery:	1 X 4-bbl.	1 X 4-bbl.	1 X 4-bbl.
Transmission:	4-speed manual, Turbo Hydra-Matic	4-speed manual, Turbo Hydra-Matic	4-speed manual, Turbo Hydra-Matic

DIMENSIONS

Wheelbase (in.):	98
Overall length (in.):	184.7
Overall height (in.):	47.8
Overall width (in.):	69.0
Track front/rear (in.):	58.7/59.5
Curb weight (lbs):	3725

1973 Selected Colors

Orange Met.	Targa Blue Met.
Millie Miglia Red	Yellow Met.
Medium Blue Met.	Blue-Green Met.

▲ Engine roar was reduced via the insertion of extra body sound deadener at strategic points, plus a new underhood insulating pad. Body mounts changed to flexible rubber/steel, and a hood extension replaced the troublesome pop-up wiper panel.

▲ With its "glassback" profile, the XP-898 styling exercise was similar to the shape of the next Corvette (which didn't arrive for 10 more years), but more like Chevy's upcoming, third-generation Camaro. Suspension and running gear, however, came from the twin-cam Cosworth Vega. Glass-reinforced plastic formed the unit body/chassis.

1974

Long lines at the gas pumps led off the year as the oil crisis continued. On April 18, the OPEC embargo was lifted, but prices stayed high when shipments resumed.

Investigation of the Watergate cover-up led to the threat of impeachment of President Nixon. On August 8, before any such move, Nixon resigned. Gerald Ford took office to finish Nixon's term. Later, Nelson Rockefeller was named vice-president.

Ford pardoned Nixon in September. Then, he proposed his economic program, W.I.N. (Whip Inflation Now). American citizens were permitted to own gold for the first time since 1933.

Newspaper heiress Patty Hearst was kidnapped by radicals and participated in a bank robbery. Dr. Henry Heimlich announced a technique to save choking victims. Hank Aaron hit his 715th home run, topping Babe Ruth's record.

•All cars have seatbelt interlock ignition systems

•Corvette's molded tail gets "soft" 5-mph rear bumper

•Volume grows to 37,502

•Some Corvettes carry rare, ultra-stiff Z07 "Off Road Suspension and Brake Package"

•Most potent small-block is the 250-bhp, 350-cid V-8

•Final year for big-block 454-cid V-8 (rated 270 bhp), and genuine dual exhausts

▲ A two-piece, body-color, urethane-sheathed rear end elbowed aside the Kamm-style tail. Created to meet five-mph bumper rules, it had a smooth, integrated look.

◄ Shoulder and lap belts were combined to create an easy-to-use three-point harness. The rearview mirror grew to 10 inches wide to give a broader view.

► More costly and plush each year, Corvettes lured a new breed of customer—one who wanted an upgraded grand tourer. Chevy promoted the car as "one of the great pleasures in life," adding that "anyone who truly loves the road . . . deserves that pleasure at least once."

Have you noticed how legends tend to improve with time?

Corvette, America's only true production sports car for the past 21 years, a legend in its time and yours, now has a handsome new impact-absorbing rear end with a resilient urethane cover. Other 1974 improvements include new exhaust resonators and tail pipes to help soften the sound, new air conditioning out-lets for improved air distribution, a wider rearview mirror inside and new color choices inside and out, and a new "Gymkhana" suspension you can order. If you've wanted a Corvette since you were a kid, you've waited long enough.

CHEVROLET MAKES SENSE FOR AMERICA. Chevrolet GM

DIMENSIONS

Wheelbase (in.):	98
Overall length (in.):	185.1
Overall height (in.):	47.8
Overall width (in.):	69.0
Track front/rear (in.):	58.7/59.5
Curb weight (lbs):	3492

▼ Complementing the front end, the new downward-tapered, energy-absorbent molded tail was less efficient at holding down the rear, but it didn't seem to hurt aerodynamics too much. The two-piece bumper had a visible center seam.

▲ The racing ban lifted, Corvettes with 427-cid V-8 power fared well at Daytona. The energy crisis of '74 put a temporary damper on racing, but within a year things at the track were back to normal. However, the Corvette had become too big and heavy to compete effectively against the purpose-built machines from Porsche and BMW. So the Corvettes had to be satisfied with continued success in SCCA. America's sports car was A-production champion from 1973 to '78 and B-production title-holder in '73 and '74. Corvettes also did well in the new sport of Autocross.

▼ Relatively modest changes produced a 'Vette that looked fresh, even though nothing more than the front, rear, scoops, and trim were new. Despite sinking industry trends, sales held strong as volume hit 37,502 units.

▲ Brochures promised that the new twin resonators (mini-mufflers) in the dual exhaust system "still deliver the growl of performance you know and like, but at a level that now lets you enjoy" the radio.

◄ The global energy crisis helped convince buyers that a balanced blend of performance teamed with handling and civility was the wisest course.

◄ Deep-pleat seats were claimed to be "canted at the edges to keep you firmly positioned behind the wheel, during hard cornering." A new option this year was a map light.

▲ A single quarter-panel scoop replaced the slatted one on previous 'Vettes. An L82 Stingray was no slouch, able to hit 60 in 7.5 seconds. The theft alarm switch moved to the left front fender.

◄ Once again, customers had three engine choices. The 350-cid V-8 came as a 195-bhp Turbo-Fire or 250-bhp L82 "for the enthusiast." In its final year, the big-block 454 Turbo-Jet made 270 bhp. Even the brochure noted the adage that "Nothing beats inches," adding that an LS4 "provides a lusty torque output."

ENGINE SPECS

1974	L48	L82	LS4
Type:	ohv V-8	ohv V-8	ohv V-8
Bore X stroke (in.):	4.00 X 3.48	4.00 X 3.48	4.25 X 4.00
Displacement (ci):	350	350	454
Compression ratio:	8.5:1	9.0:1	8.25:1
Horsepower @ rpm (bhp):	195 @ 4400	250 @ 5200	270 @ 4400
Torque @ rpm (lbs/feet):	275 @ 2800	285 @ 4000	380 @ 2800
Fuel Delivery:	1 X 4-bbl.	1 X 4-bbl.	1 X 4-bbl.
Transmission:	4-speed manual, Turbo Hydra-Matic	4-speed manual, Turbo Hydra-Matic	4-speed manual, Turbo Hydra-Matic

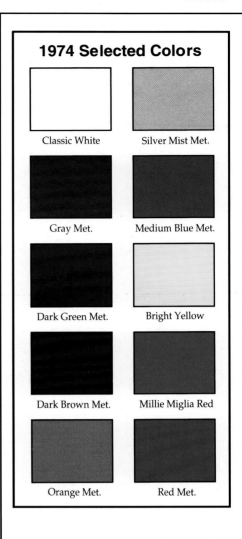

1974 Selected Colors

Classic White

Silver Mist Met.

Gray Met.

Medium Blue Met.

Dark Green Met.

Bright Yellow

Dark Brown Met.

Millie Miglia Red

Orange Met.

Red Met.

▲ A multi-louvered radiator helped keep a 'Vette cool in city traffic. For only seven bucks, an FE7 Gymkhana suspension offered higher-rate springs and firmer shocks, giving tighter handling. Gymkhanas weren't recommended for general driving.

▼ This was the last year for engines that ran on leaded gas as well as for a true dual, non-catalytic converter exhaust system. A continuing sleeper in the option bin was the Z07 Off Road Suspension and Brake package at $400.

Three top men in the Nixon White House—H.R. Haldeman, John Ehrlichman, and John Mitchell—received prison sentences for their part in the Watergate cover-up. President Ford survived two assassination attempts.

Saigon, the capital of South Vietnam, fell to the Vietcong.

The Supreme Court ruled that a criminal defendant may conduct his own defense. William O. Douglas resigned his seat after 36 years on the Court.

Early in the year, the U.S. Treasury auctioned off a portion of its gold supply. In November, six major Western nations met for the first economic summit.

Apollo-Soyuz, the first joint American-Soviet space mission, took place in July.

Sony VCRs hit the stores. Top movies this year included *Jaws* and *Nashville*.

• Major automakers turn to rebates to boost sales

• Catalytic converters installed on all Chevrolets

• Corvettes change little in appearance, but hold new bladder-type fuel cells and subtle suspension revisions

• Final Chevy convertibles built, including Corvette's

• 350-cid V-8 rates 165 bhp in standard tune, or 205 bhp in optional L82 dress

• Engines get breakerless electronic ignition

• SCCA Trans-Am champion is John Greenwood

CORVETTE '75

Here's this year's version of last year's "Best All-Around Car," as selected by readers of *Car and Driver* magazine. Corvette makes excitement make sense.

CHEVROLET MAKES SENSE FOR AMERICA.

▲ Chevy's promised "excitement" dwindled further as 'Vette horsepowers hit their low point. Prices had been rising steadily, reaching $6857 for the roadster and $7117 for the coupe. However, output edged up to 38,465, including only 4629 roadsters.

▲ Few obvious physical changes were evident in this year's Stingray, but it would be the final year for the Corvette roadster—for another decade, that is. The standard 350-cid V-8's output shrunk to 165 horsepower. The L82 option gave an extra 40 horses (205 bhp). Alas, the 454 big-block was dropped early in the model year.

◀ This year's rear bumper was a seamless, resilient one-piece unit. New features included breakerless electronic ignition and electronic tach drive.

▼ Small, black-painted extrusions gave bumpers extra parking-lot protection. Traditional dual exhausts were replaced by separate manifolds routed to one catalytic converter, then to twin tailpipes.

▼ Threatened government rollover standards never came to pass, but they helped seal the fate of all Chevrolet convertibles, including Corvette's. A headlights-on warning buzzer was now required. Noses held no real bumper, but a minor impact would be cushioned by the resilient honeycomb substructure. Outside mirrors gained an inch in width.

ENGINE SPECS

1975	L48	L82
Type:	ohv V-8	ohv V-8
Bore X stroke (in.):	4.00 X 3.48	4.00 X 3.48
Displacement (ci)	350	350
Compression ratio:	8.5:1	9.0:1
Horsepower @ rpm (bhp):	165 @ 3800	205 @ 4800
Torque @ rpm (lbs/feet):	255 @ 2400	255 @ 3600
Fuel Delivery:	1 X 4-bbl.	1 X 4-bbl.
Transmission:	4-speed manual, Turbo Hydra-Matic	4-speed manual, Turbo Hydra-Matic

DIMENSIONS

Wheelbase (in.):	98
Overall length (in.):	185.2
Overall height (in.):	48.1
Overall width (in.):	69.0
Track front/rear (in.):	58.7/59.5
Curb weight (lbs):	3660

▲ Chevy promoted the new "Efficiency System" with Early Fuel Evaporation and outside air carburetion, helping Corvettes "run leaner (more economically), cleaner, and save money."

▼ Gymkhana and Off-Road suspensions again were offered. All windows contained Soft-Ray tinted glass, and seating areas were upholstered in standard vinyl or Custom leather.

1975 Selected Colors

Classic White | Bright Blue Met. | Steel Blue Met. | Bright Green Met.

Bright Yellow | Medium Saddle | Flame Red | Millie Miglia Red

▼ GM design chief Bill Mitchell called the Mulsanne the "greatest Stingray ever." Styling was described as having "much animation." Created in the late '60's, it was updated with "soft" bumpers and high mirrors. Powered by a potent LT1 engine, it served as the pace car for Can Am races. Loaded with scoops, fins, and spoilers, the Mulsanne was most notable for the wideview rear-facing periscope in its fixed roof, instead of a mirror.

▼ All engines now ran on no-lead gas. A luggage rack was a practical accessory. A welcome addition was a bladder-style fuel cell.

1976

Celebration of the nation's Bicentennial culminated in July 4th festivities. In a close race, Georgia governor Jimmy Carter defeated Gerald Ford for the presidency, with Walter Mondale as vice-president.

Richard J. Daley, long-time mayor of Chicago, died, as did multimillionaire recluse Howard Hughes.

Americans captured all Nobel prizes (except Peace) for the first time. Author Tom Wolfe proclaimed 1976 the middle of the "Me Decade."

"Legionnaire's" disease killed 28 in Philadelphia. Two young engineering wizards, Steven Jobs and Steven Wozniak, started the Apple computer company in a garage with $1300 in capital. Cadillac built its last Eldorado convertible, and the first supersonic Concorde landed in Washington.

On the silver screen, *All the President's Men* portrayed the Watergate investigation, while *Rocky* chronicled the rise of a prizefighter.

• Except for new rear badge and partial-steel underbody, Corvette change is minimal

• Coupe as the only body style is first time in 'Vette history

• Horsepowers on rise again after bottoming in 1975

• Engine selections include L48 180-bhp, 350-cid V-8 or optional L82 with 210 bhp

• Corvette sales hit record, with 46,558 coupes built

▲ High-back, textured-vinyl bucket seats wore pleated, saddle-stitched panels. Map pockets were ahead of the passenger, while the driver faced a 160-mph speedometer.

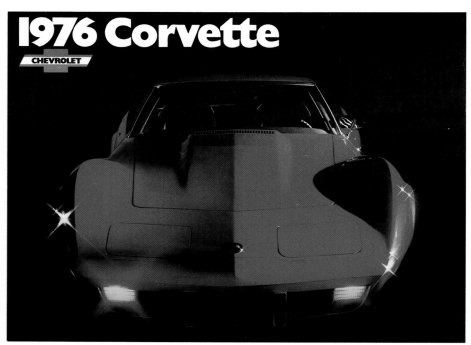

1976 Corvette
CHEVROLET

▲ Buyers were encouraged to view Corvette as "an automotive investment," and an "escape machine." Full instrumentation continued, despite the car's continuing move upscale.

ENGINE SPECS

1976	L48	L82
Type:	ohv V-8	ohv V-8
Bore X stroke (in.):	4.00 X 3.48	4.00 X 3.48
Displacement (ci):	350	350
Compression ratio:	8.5:1	9.0:1
Horsepower @ rpm (bhp):	180 @ 4000	210 @ 5200
Torque @ rpm (lbs/feet):	270 @ 2400	255 @ 3600
Fuel Delivery:	1 X 4-bbl.	1 X 4-bbl.
Transmission:	4-speed manual, Turbo Hydra-Matic	4-speed manual, Turbo Hydra-Matic

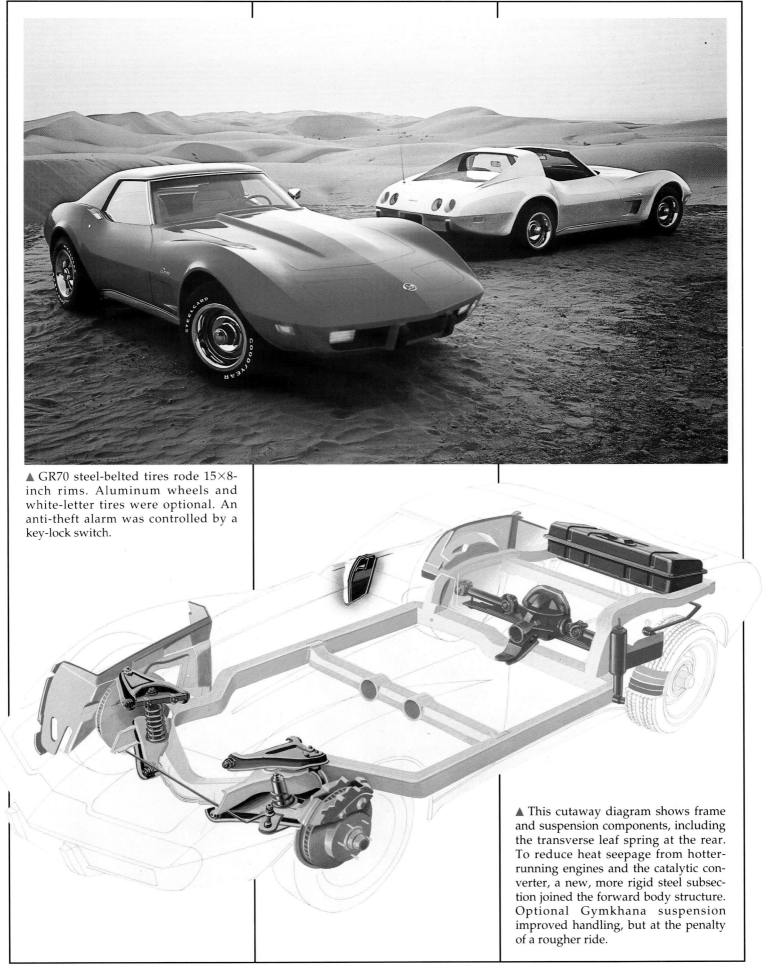

▲ GR70 steel-belted tires rode 15×8-inch rims. Aluminum wheels and white-letter tires were optional. An anti-theft alarm was controlled by a key-lock switch.

▲ This cutaway diagram shows frame and suspension components, including the transverse leaf spring at the rear. To reduce heat seepage from hotter-running engines and the catalytic converter, a new, more rigid steel subsection joined the forward body structure. Optional Gymkhana suspension improved handling, but at the penalty of a rougher ride.

▲ Critics complained that mid-1970s 'Vettes had grown "soft." Defenders explained that the car was merely evolving into a grand tourer.

DIMENSIONS

Wheelbase (in.):	98
Overall length (in.):	185.2
Overall height (in.):	48.0
Overall width (in.):	69.0
Track front/rear (in.):	58.7/59.5
Curb weight (lbs):	3608

1976 Selected Colors

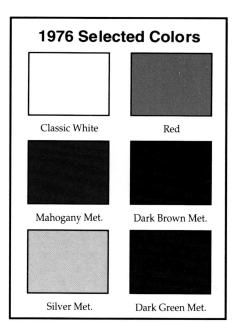

Classic White

Red

Mahogany Met.

Dark Brown Met.

Silver Met.

Dark Green Met.

▲ This year's smaller-diameter, four-spoke steering wheel was borrowed from the subcompact Vega GT. Behind the seats sat three stowage bins.

▲ Crossed flags were a continuing Corvette theme. When urged, an L82 with automatic could dash to 60 mph in 7.1 seconds.

▲ One clue to the '76 model was a new Corvette badge, between the taillights.

▲ The base L48 350-cid V-8 gained 15 horsepower for a total of 180. The L82 option rose to 210 bhp. Both now drew air through an intake ahead of the radiator, rather than at the cowl.

▲ Fake air-extractor vents departed from the rear deck, while bumper trim was altered slightly. Roof panels offered greater "buttoned-up security," but came off in less than a minute.

▲ A single switch caused the headlights to rotate open and illuminate.

▶ List price jumped to $7605, and production leaped to 46,558 due to a recovering market.

President Carter pardoned Vietnam-era draft evaders, fulfilling a campaign pledge. He later described the energy crisis as "the moral equivalent of war," calling for reduction in consumption. Half the public believed there was no crisis.

America agreed to sign the Panama Canal over to Panama by the year 2000. The $8 billion TransAlaska pipeline was completed, sending oil from the North Slope to Valdez. In May, the space shuttle *Enterprise* made its first test flight, riding piggyback on a Boeing 747.

The minimum wage was hiked to $2.65 an hour, scheduled to rise to $3.35 in 1981, and the Department of Energy was created. Imports took nearly one-fifth of car sales, and GM debuted a number of diesel autos.

Rock idol Elvis Presley died August 16. Alex Haley won a special Pulitzer Prize for his book, *Roots,* and the TV version drew 80 million viewers.

• New Corvette console holds simpler climate controls

• Leather-trimmed sport steering wheel and leather upholstery become standard along with power brakes/ steering

• Stingray name deleted

• Ratings for 350-cid V-8 remain the same: 180/210 bhp

• Production rises to 49,213, despite $1043 price hike

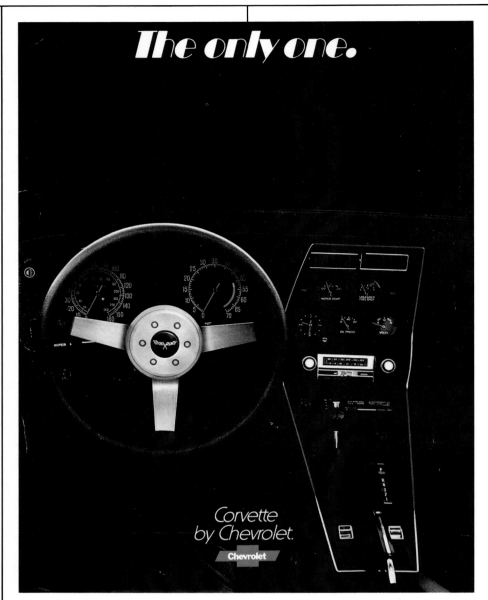

The only one.

Corvette by Chevrolet.

Chevrolet

▲ After all these years, Corvette was still "America's only true production sports car." Power steering and brakes became standard, as the price hit $8648.

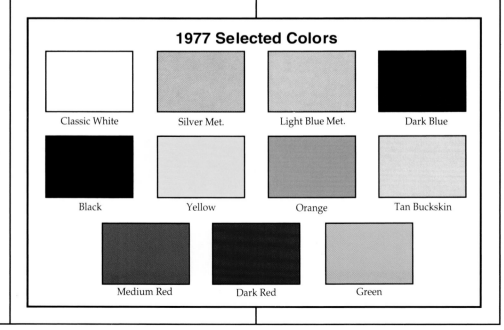

1977 Selected Colors

Classic White	Silver Met.	Light Blue Met.	Dark Blue
Black	Yellow	Orange	Tan Buckskin
Medium Red	Dark Red	Green	

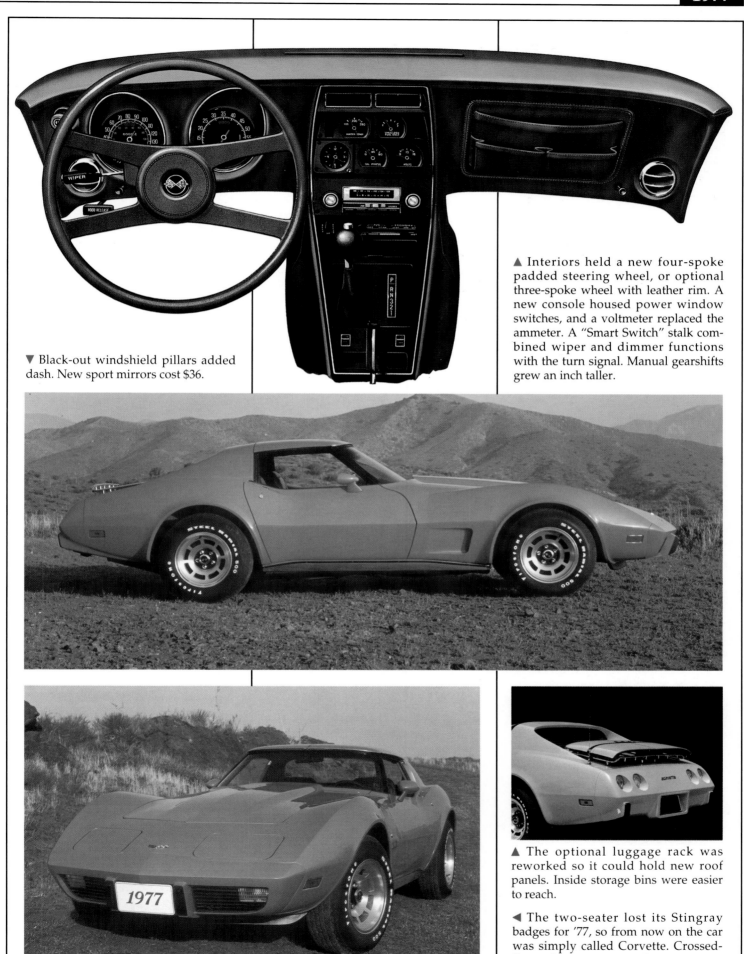

▼ Black-out windshield pillars added dash. New sport mirrors cost $36.

▲ Interiors held a new four-spoke padded steering wheel, or optional three-spoke wheel with leather rim. A new console housed power window switches, and a voltmeter replaced the ammeter. A "Smart Switch" stalk combined wiper and dimmer functions with the turn signal. Manual gearshifts grew an inch taller.

▲ The optional luggage rack was reworked so it could hold new roof panels. Inside storage bins were easier to reach.

◄ The two-seater lost its Stingray badges for '77, so from now on the car was simply called Corvette. Crossed-flag emblems were new this year.

▲ With its big hood bulge, a '77 Corvette cut quite an impressive profile. Despite higher prices, production set a record at 49,213. Custom-level interior trim with leather upholstery was now standard; otherwise, buyers could elect cloth seats with hide bolsters.

▶ Once again, the 350-cid V-8 came in two horsepower ratings: 180 or 210. Only 6148 cars carried the optional L82 engine, and just 5043 came with the M20 four-speed gearbox. Another 2060 cars had the M26 close-ratio unit. New stainless steel covers on mufflers helped protect against corrosion.

DIMENSIONS

Wheelbase (in.):	98
Overall length (in.):	185.2
Overall height (in.):	48.0
Overall width (in.):	69.0
Track front/rear (in.):	58.7/59.5
Curb weight (lbs):	3595

ENGINE SPECS

1977	L48	L82
Type:	ohv V-8	ohv V-8
Bore X stroke (in.):	4.00 X 3.48	4.00 X 3.48
Displacement (ci):	350	350
Compression ratio:	8.5:1	9.0:1
Horsepower @ rpm (bhp):	180 @ 4000	210 @ 5200
Torque @ rpm (lbs/feet):	270 @ 2400	255 @ 3600
Fuel Delivery:	1 X 4-bbl.	1 X 4-bbl.
Transmission:	4-speed manual, Turbo Hydra-Matic	4-speed manual, Turbo Hydra-Matic

◀ Luggage space was still scanty, so a rack was well worth $73 to many buyers. Bold vertical rectangular exhausts added to the Corvette's still-tough image. With manual shift and an L82 engine, a 'Vette could hit 60 mph in 7.0 seconds or less.

▲ Most of the changes for '77 were hidden, such as the installation of a steel hood reinforcement. Chevrolet's goal during these years was to create a refined cruiser. An AM/FM stereo radio with built-in cassette deck was offered for the first time, as was cruise control.

▶ Deep-tinted glass roof panels were offered at the start of the season, but canceled because of a dispute with the supplier over sales rights. They would become a real option in '78, delivered by another supplier. The half-millionth Corvette was built in March 1977.

1978

President Carter signed the Nuclear Non-Proliferation Act, restricting the export of fissionable materials. Also, Carter's Camp David accords began, intended to bring peace to the Middle East.

Californians passed Proposition 13, gaining huge cuts in property taxes. In the Bakke case, the Supreme Court ruled fixed racial quotas unconstitutional.

At Jonestown, in Guyana, hundreds of followers of the Rev. Jim Jones were killed in a ritualistic mass murder and suicide. For the first time since the Depression, a U.S. city—Cleveland—went into default.

Dallas, the prime-time soap opera, debuted on TV. Muhammad Ali captured the heavyweight boxing title for the third time.

OPEC raised oil prices by 14.5 percent in December, leading eventually to a second oil crisis.

- All '78 Corvettes display new fastback roof treatment

- Marking its 25th birthday, Corvette paces the Indianapolis 500 race

- Indy Pace Car and Silver Anniversary Corvettes sold

- 6200 Pace Car Replicas painted black/silver with special spoilers

- Anniversary model wears two-tone silver paint

- 350-cid V-8 is rated 185 or 220 horsepower

- 47,667 coupes built, including special editions

▲ This year's dashboard held a squared-up housing for the speedometer and tach to match the console changes from the previous year. A glovebox with a real door replaced the old map pockets. Door panels were redone, with new armrests and integral pulls, and the wiper/washer control moved back to the dashboard.

▲ Abandoning the former "flying buttress" sail panels, Chevrolet installed a large, compound-curved back window to create a fastback roofline. In addition to improving rearward visibility, the new window added needed luggage space. However, the glass was fixed. Silver Anniversary emblems on the nose and rear deck marked the car's 25th year.

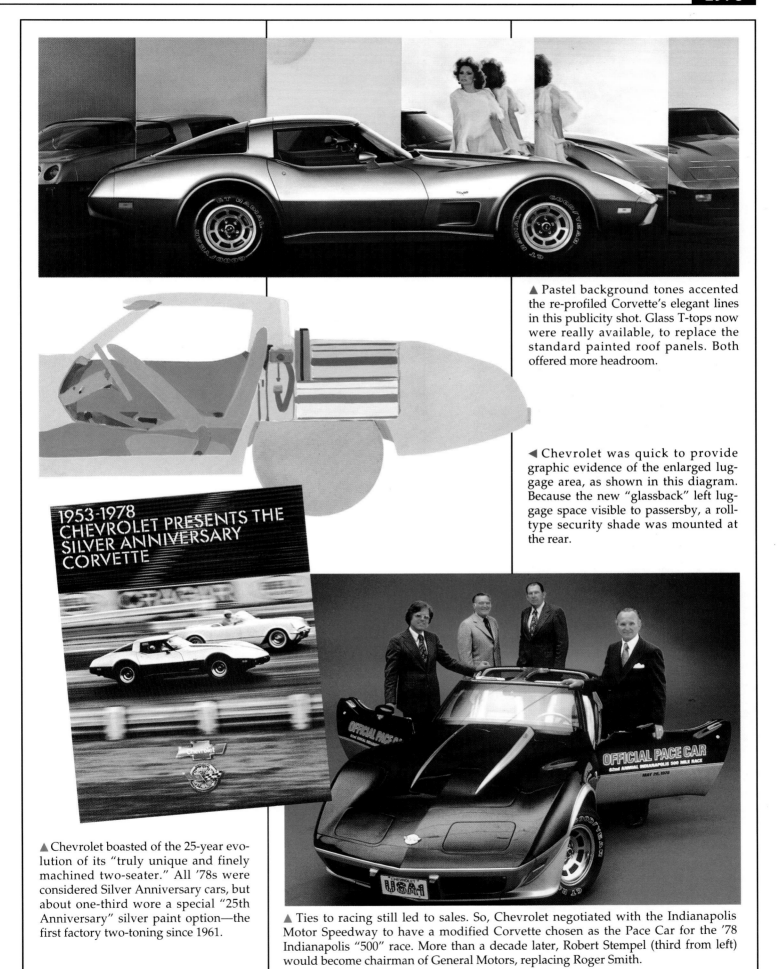

▲ Pastel background tones accented the re-profiled Corvette's elegant lines in this publicity shot. Glass T-tops now were really available, to replace the standard painted roof panels. Both offered more headroom.

◄ Chevrolet was quick to provide graphic evidence of the enlarged luggage area, as shown in this diagram. Because the new "glassback" left luggage space visible to passersby, a roll-type security shade was mounted at the rear.

1953-1978 CHEVROLET PRESENTS THE SILVER ANNIVERSARY CORVETTE

▲ Chevrolet boasted of the 25-year evolution of its "truly unique and finely machined two-seater." All '78s were considered Silver Anniversary cars, but about one-third wore a special "25th Anniversary" silver paint option—the first factory two-toning since 1961.

▲ Ties to racing still led to sales. So, Chevrolet negotiated with the Indianapolis Motor Speedway to have a modified Corvette chosen as the Pace Car for the '78 Indianapolis "500" race. More than a decade later, Robert Stempel (third from left) would become chairman of General Motors, replacing Roger Smith.

▲ Because Chevrolet had no all-new model ready to mark Corvette's 25th year, it needed to modify the existing car. The wraparound back window, a low-cost alteration that freshened appearance, improved visibility and lended a more airy feel.

ENGINE SPECS

1978	L48	L82
Type:	ohv V-8	ohv V-8
Bore X stroke (in.):	4.00 X 3.48	4.00 X 3.48
Displacement (ci):	350	350
Compression ratio:	8.5:1	8.9:1
Horsepower @ rpm (bhp):	185 @ 4000[1]	220 @ 5200
Torque @ rpm (lbs/feet):	270 @ 2400	260 @ 3600
Fuel Delivery:	1 X 4-bbl.	1 X 4-bbl.
Transmission:	4-speed manual, Turbo Hydra-Matic	4-speed manual, Turbo Hydra-Matic

[1] 175 bhp in California

DIMENSIONS

Wheelbase (in.):	98
Overall length (in.):	185.2
Overall height (in.):	48.0
Overall width (in.):	69.0
Track front/rear (in.):	58.7/59.5
Curb weight (lbs):	3595

1978 Selected Colors

Classic White Silver Met.

Light Blue Yellow

Light Beige Red

Mahogany Met. Dark Blue Met.

▲ This year's coupe had a base price of $9645, or nearly $1000 more than 1977—which itself had seen a similar hike. The B2Z paint option, adding $399, included a silver metallic upper body, charcoal silver lower body, plus pinstripe separation and accents. Aluminum wheels and dual sport mirrors were mandatory.

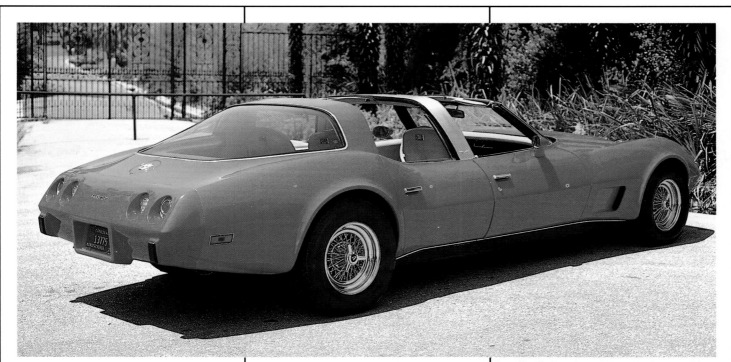

▲ California Custom Coach created this bizarre stretched four-door conversion of a Corvette two-seater.

◀ Adding space for two more passengers may have been practical, but the long 'Vette lost its sports-car look.

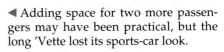

▲ From front or rear, little evidence showed that this 'Vette had four doors.

◀ Nothing differed much inside the four-door conversion, which sported T-top panels over both front and rear seats.

129

▲ Enough "Limited Edition Indy Pace Car Replicas" were built so every Chevy dealer could get one. They contained special silver seats and wore black-over-silver paint, accented with red pinstriping. A rear spoiler wrapped down to mid-body height.

OFFICIAL PACE CAR
62nd ANNUAL INDIANAPOLIS 500 MILE RACE
MAY 28, 1978

▲ The Pace Car Replica was actually an option package—RPO Z78. List price was $13,653, $4008 more than a base coupe, but included a host of extras. The door decals were shipped inside the car, leaving the buyer the option of installing them.

▶ Emblems at front and rear commemorated the Silver Anniversary (1953-1978). A dual-snorkel air cleaner and low-restriction exhaust improved performance of the L82 engine to 220 bhp. Base rating was 185 bhp (175 in some areas).

▲ Because of its new airy rear window, the '78 Corvette offered better rear-quarter visibility. The luggage area not only was larger but easier to reach, with enough space for storage of the roof panels. A hinged backlight would have been nicer yet—but that would have to wait until the next generation.

▲ The Limited Edition Pace Car Replica sported a wraparound chin spoiler that blended into wheel wells, similar to the Pontiac Firebird Trans Am. Its thin-shell seats previewed seating that would be standard in all '79 Corvettes.

▲ For an extra $525, the L82 edition of the 350-cid V-8 put out 220 bhp. A close-ratio four-speed returned as an exclusive option for the L82.

▲ Limited Edition badges rode front fenders of Pace Car replicas. Standard equipment included an AM/FM stereo with eight-track tape player or CB unit.

▲ The Pace Car decal package, which included the winged Speedway logo, was not installed at the factory. Most "Indy 'Vettes" went for well over the sticker price.

◀ Silver Anniversary Corvettes cost an extra $399 for paint alone. Since they were favorites of car thieves, the standard anti-theft system was wired into the lift-out roof panels—which had an unfortunate habit of disappearing from unprotected cars on dark nights. The fuel tank grew from 17 to 24 gallons, and "aggressive" 60-series (225/60R15) tires were available for the first time. Corvettes had a new temporary spare tire and the option of an FE7 Gymkhana suspension ($41), which gave the car a suppleness roughly equivalent to that of a tank.

Following President Carter's 1978 Camp David accords, Egyptian President Anwar Sadat and Israeli Prime Minister Menachem Begin signed a peace treaty. Carter announced a plan to build the MX missile.

Inflation was rising—the Consumer Price Index saw its biggest jump in 33 years. Congress approved a $1.5 billion loan to Chrysler.

OPEC raised oil prices sharply, triggering another crisis. At the Tokyo "energy summit," the U.S. agreed to limit imports.

In March, a cooling system defect led to radiation leakage at Pennsylvania's Three-Mile Island nuclear plant. Tom Wolfe published *The Right Stuff*, chronicling the lives of early astronauts.

The U.S. and Soviets agreed to the SALT II treaty, limiting strategic missiles. In Iran, the Islamic revolution began, led by Ayatollah Khomeini. On November 4, Iranian students seized the U.S. Embassy in Teheran, taking 90 hostages.

• New Corvette logo features elongated crossed-flags

• AM/FM radio now standard; bolt-on spoilers optional

• Low-restriction exhaust increases output of L48 and optional L82 engines to 195 and 225 bhp, respectively

• New seats are similar to those in 1978 Indy Pace Car

• Corvette sales set record, despite big hike to $10,220; total of 53,807 built

Corvette
Chevrolet

1979

▲ Refined in handling and comfort, Chevy's "magic machine to whisk you away from everyday" added horses to its 350-cid (5.7-liter) V-8, plus improved cold-engine driveability.

▲ Changes were few and evolutionary, but output set another record at 53,807. The base engine gained 10 horsepower (now 195), by adopting the L82's more efficient twin-snorkel air cleaner. Meanwhile, the L82 option got an extra 5 (now 225 bhp).

▲ Crossed-flag insignias at the front and rear replaced the silver anniversary badges from '78.

DIMENSIONS	
Wheelbase (in.):	98
Overall length (in.):	185.2
Overall height (in.):	48.0
Overall width (in.):	69.0
Track front/rear (in.):	58.7/59.5
Curb weight (lbs):	3655

▲ High-back bucket seats had debuted on the '78 Pace Car Replica. Seatbacks folded flat (level with the luggage floor) and had differential inertia locks, but did not recline. Fiberglass-reinforced plastic saved about 24 pounds in the seats.

▼ Tungsten-halogen headlamps were phased in. A new option now included front/rear spoilers.

▲ Engine modifications and a shorter axle ratio (from 3.08:1 to 3.55:1) gave automatic 'Vettes better response off the line. An AM/FM radio was now standard.

▼ Larger-diameter exhaust with open-flow mufflers eased engine breathing. A new "4+1 Quick Change" five-speed gearbox was marketed by racer Doug Nash—who later produced a transmission for the next generation Corvette.

1979 Selected Colors

Classic White	Light Blue	Red	Silver Met.
Dark Green Met.	Medium Blue	Light Beige	Yellow
Dark Brown Met.	Dark Blue Met.	Black	Dark Red

▲ Starting late in 1979 and into 1980, American Custom Industries of Sylvania, Ohio, created a small number of Duntov Turbos. After tearing off the factory body, ACI added Bilstein shocks and wide wheels with massive tires.

▲ Inside, the Duntov Turbo was less startling than its all-new body panels suggested. Among other modifications, steering was tightened. ACI produced a variety of custom 'Vettes to customer specs, priced to $45,000 for a race-ready version.

▶ The Duntov Turbo's fiberglass convertible body took its basic styling themes from Corvette, but wore wider fenders, a modest rear spoiler, and fixed rectangular headlights. Red striping accented the body crease and rear panel.

▲ As the special Duntov Turbo logo spells out, just 200 turbocharged "Limited Editions" were planned, although it is doubtful many were actually produced.

▲ To complete the transformation, a Turbo International blower was bolted onto the original L48 engine.

ENGINE SPECS		
1979	L48	L82
Type:	ohv V-8	ohv V-8
Bore X stroke (in.):	4.00 X 3.48	4.00 X 3.48
Displacement (ci):	350	350
Compression ratio:	8.5:1	8.9:1
Horsepower @ rpm (bhp):	185 @ 4000	220 @ 5200
Torque @ rpm (lbs/feet):	270 @ 2400	260 @ 3600
Fuel Delivery:	1 X 4-bbl.	1 X 4-bbl.
Transmission:	4-speed manual, Turbo Hydra-Matic	4-speed manual, Turbo Hydra-Matic

In January, President Carter banned the sale of grain to the Soviets in retribution for their invasion of Afghanistan. On April 15, Carter ordered a military expedition to rescue hostages taken by Iran, but the attempt failed.

Mount St. Helens erupted on May 18 in Washington state. United Auto Workers President Douglas Fraser took a seat on Chrysler's board—a "first" for a union leader.

The U.S. and 50 other nations boycotted the Summer Olympics in the Soviet Union. After a flurry of strikes in Poland, the "Solidarity" movement was formed.

Former actor and California governor Ronald Reagan defeated Jimmy Carter for the presidency.

An era seemed to come to an end on December 8 with the fatal shooting of ex-Beatle John Lennon.

• Corvettes earn a more contemporary look with front/rear spoilers that aid high-speed aerodynamics

• Weight cut through greater use of plastic and aluminum components

• New equipment includes tilt-telescopic steering wheel and air conditioning

• 350-cid V-8 engine is rated 190 bhp; 230 bhp is optional

• Smaller 305-cid V-8 used in California Corvettes, rated 180 bhp

• Production drops sharply, to 40,614 Corvettes

▲ The big news for the Corvette in 1980 was less—250 lbs. less. All a part of GM's quest to meet Corporate Average Fuel Economy (CAFE) standards. The front air dam and rear spoiler were reshaped and made standard, smoothly integrated into bumper covers.

▲ In addition to a more steeply raked grille, the front end held a new fiberglass face bar and two fiberglass corner braces, for marked reductions in weight. This year's four-speed manual gearbox had wider gear ratios and an energy-saving lock-up torque converter clutch that went into automatic transmissions (except in California).

▲ An aluminum intake manifold (formerly on the L82) was now standard on the base L48 engine. Emissions tuning cut its output by 5 bhp, to 190 at 4400 rpm. Meanwhile, the optional L82 gained 5 bhp, now rated 230. Californians had to be content with a smaller (305-cid), 180-bhp V-8, offered only with automatic transmission.

▲ Nineteen-eighty was a year for subtle interior changes, including the relocation of the power door-lock button; a single combined storage compartment behind the seats replaced the former twin separate units. The battery remained in a separate cubby behind the driver.

▲ Imitators of Chevy's "legendary classic" were many, the sales brochure declared, but "none of them catch your eye with such striking authority."

▲ Both Chevrolet and outside firms experimented with turbo-powered Corvettes. Turbocharging was an easy way to add horsepower without major engine modifications.

▶ For better or worse, turbos would never become part of Corvette production history, except when added by aftermarket firms. This was one of several turbo 'Vettes created by GM.

▲ With that long hood bulge and flanking louvers, something special just had to be lurking inside. In this case, it was one of a series of turbocharged engines developed by GM in an effort to meet CAFE regulations and provide more power.

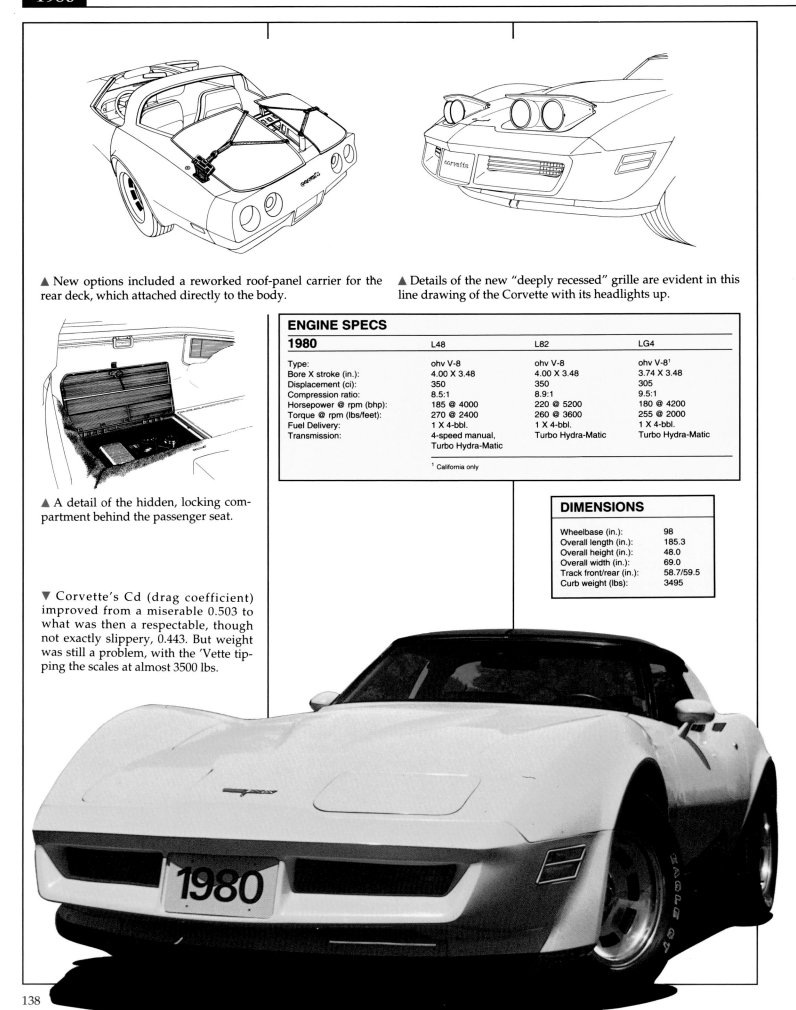

▲ New options included a reworked roof-panel carrier for the rear deck, which attached directly to the body.

▲ Details of the new "deeply recessed" grille are evident in this line drawing of the Corvette with its headlights up.

▲ A detail of the hidden, locking compartment behind the passenger seat.

▼ Corvette's Cd (drag coefficient) improved from a miserable 0.503 to what was then a respectable, though not exactly slippery, 0.443. But weight was still a problem, with the 'Vette tipping the scales at almost 3500 lbs.

ENGINE SPECS

1980	L48	L82	LG4
Type:	ohv V-8	ohv V-8	ohv V-8[1]
Bore X stroke (in.):	4.00 X 3.48	4.00 X 3.48	3.74 X 3.48
Displacement (ci):	350	350	305
Compression ratio:	8.5:1	8.9:1	9.5:1
Horsepower @ rpm (bhp):	185 @ 4000	220 @ 5200	180 @ 4200
Torque @ rpm (lbs/feet):	270 @ 2400	260 @ 3600	255 @ 2000
Fuel Delivery:	1 X 4-bbl.	1 X 4-bbl.	1 X 4-bbl.
Transmission:	4-speed manual, Turbo Hydra-Matic	Turbo Hydra-Matic	Turbo Hydra-Matic

[1] California only

DIMENSIONS

Wheelbase (in.):	98
Overall length (in.):	185.3
Overall height (in.):	48.0
Overall width (in.):	69.0
Track front/rear (in.):	58.7/59.5
Curb weight (lbs):	3495

▼ Corvettes now had standard air conditioning, a tilt/telescope steering wheel, remote mirrors, power windows, and time-delay lighting. Sadly, per government rule, the speedometer stopped at 85 mph.

▶ Functional front-fender air exhaust vents added vertical black louvers; crossed-flags emblems departed.

▲ This year's modest restyling also boosted fuel economy a bit, though drivers couldn't expect much more than 14-15 mpg in ordinary use. Weight cuts were achieved by using more aluminum and plastic parts, including an aluminum differential housing and front-frame cross-member.

▲ Chevrolet claimed that the slippery 1980 Corvette had a "recognizably new, aerodynamic appearance." The hood, in particular, showed a lower profile. Rally wheels with trim rings and center caps held P225/70R15 steel-belted radial tires. An L82 with four-speed hit 60 mph in 7.7 seconds or less.

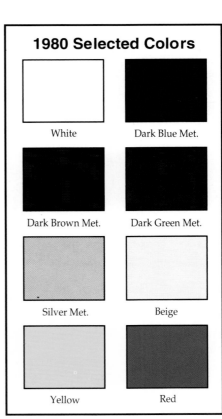

1980 Selected Colors

White	Dark Blue Met.
Dark Brown Met.	Dark Green Met.
Silver Met.	Beige
Yellow	Red

1981

Minutes after Ronald Reagan took office as president, 52 hostages were freed by Iran. In February, he proposed an economic plan to cut the budget and reduce taxes.

In March, Reagan was shot and wounded by John Hinckley. Reagan's press secretary, James Brady, suffered a severe head injury. A month later, Reagan lifted the embargo against grain sales to the Soviets.

The space shuttle *Columbia* orbited earth and returned to the desert. Martial law was declared in Poland, and "Solidarity" banned.

In August, Reagan fired striking air traffic controllers. In a turnaround from his campaign promise, he declared that a balanced budget by 1984 could not be attained.

Sandra Day O'Connor took a seat as the first female U.S. Supreme Court Justice, and IBM introduced its first "PC".

•Corvette loses more weight

•Fiberglass-reinforced plastic rear leaf spring installed on Corvettes with automatic and base suspension

•Only one engine offered: 350-cid V-8 with 190 bhp

•Production moves to plant in Bowling Green, Kentucky

•'Vette sales remain strong, in grim year for Detroit

•Only 6.2 million cars built in the U.S. this year—a 20-year low

▲ "No other American car," the sales brochure insisted, "looks like or stirs the spirit like Corvette. . . . This is what a sports car was meant to be."

▼ Weight reduction continued as a top priority, led by a fiberglass-reinforced plastic monoleaf transverse rear spring. Installed on cars with automatic and base suspension, it saved 33 pounds. Even though the price crossed the $15,000 mark, 40,606 Corvettes were built.

◄ An improved theft alarm with starter-interrupt could be armed via the driver's door lock. A lockup torque-converter clutch (now available in 50 states) gave automatics a direct link in second/third gears.

▲ The Turbo Vette 3 engineering exercise carried an all-aluminum 350-cid V-8 with throttle-body fuel injection. An Air Research turbocharger boosted power by about 30 percent.

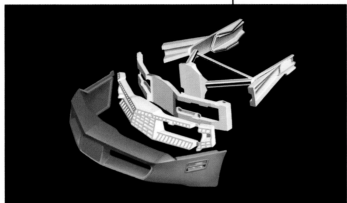

◄ The front-end assembly was strong and light. A single L81 edition of the 350-cid V-8 made 190 bhp. An auxiliary electric fan allowed a smaller engine-driven fan that cut noise.

▲ Weight-saving tricks included the use of thinner glass, plus adoption of a tubular stainless-steel exhaust manifold and black-accented magnesium engine rocker covers. Some 8995 '81 Corvettes were built at Chevrolet's new plant in Kentucky.

1980 Selected Colors

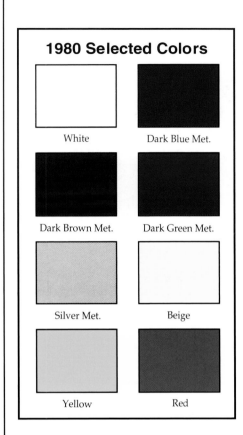

White	Dark Blue Met.
Dark Brown Met.	Dark Green Met.
Silver Met.	Beige
Yellow	Red

▲Interiors had a standard quartz clock, and could get an optional six-way power driver's seat for $173. All radios now used electronic tuning. As well, all GM engines got Computer Command Control to cut emissions and increase fuel economy.

ENGINE SPECS

1981	L81
Type:	ohv V-8
Bore X stroke (in.):	4.00 X 3.48
Displacement (ci):	350
Compression ratio:	8.2:1
Horsepower @ rpm (bhp):	190 @ 4200
Torque @ rpm (lbs/feet):	280 @ 1600
Fuel Delivery:	1 X 4-bbl.
Transmission:	4-speed manual, Turbo Hydra-Matic

DIMENSIONS

Wheelbase (in.):	98
Overall length (in.):	185.3
Overall height (in.):	48.0
Overall width (in.):	69.0
Track front/rear (in.):	58.7/59.5
Curb weight (lbs):	3345

▲At the new Bowling Green plant, online in June '81, an automated paint shop could apply durable enamels and new "clearcoat" final finishes, rather than traditional lacquer. This allowed use of metallics, and offered added durability.

Economic recession continued, with unemployment hitting 10.8 percent in November—its highest level since the Great Depression. A seven-year anti-trust action resulted in the break-up of mammoth AT&T.

In April, the U.S. barred private travel to Cuba. The nation's biggest anti-nuclear rally took place in New York City in June. U.S. Marines landed in Lebanon as part of a multi-national force. Argentina captured the British-ruled Falkland Islands, but lost them to Britain after a six-week war.

The Vietnam Veterans Memorial, designed by architectural student Maya Yang Lin, was dedicated in November. The Equal Rights Amendment failed to pass in the final three states needed for ratification.

EPCOT (Experimental Prototype Community of Tomorrow) opened alongside Disney World. *USA Today*, a nationwide newspaper, debuted.

•Cross-Fire Injection is introduced as standard equipment—first Corvette "fuelie" since 1965

•Twin throttle-body injectors push standard 5.7-liter (350-cid) V-8 to 200 horsepower

•For first time since 1954, all Corvettes have automatic transmissions

•6759 "Collector Edition" 'Vettes built with lift-up hatch, priced at $22,538

•18,648 regular coupes produced, at $18,290

▲ Because of its new drivetrain, Chevy called the '82 model "an enthusiast's kind of Corvette." It was also "a most civilized one . . . [but] with the sassy-souled gusto of its predecessors." Front fenders carried "cross-fire injection" badges to announce the arrival of Corvette's new twin throttle-body fuel injection system.

▲ Priced at $22,538, the '82 Collector Edition became the first 'Vette to crack the $20,000 barrier. To discourage the building of bogus Collector Edition cars out of regular Corvettes, Chevrolet wisely fitted special vehicle ID plates.

▲ The Collector Edition featured a flip-up rear window, silver-beige metallic paint accented by gradient-tint, and shadow-like contrasting paint stripes on the hood and body sides. Also included were cloisonne emblems and bronze-tint roof panels. Finned cast-aluminum wheels were reminiscent of those first seen on the '63 Sting Ray.

▶ A transition car, the '82 carried a new drivetrain in the old body. Because of the weak economy and expectation of a new model, output of the last "big 'Vettes" fell to 25,407 units—the lowest since 1967. Only 6759 were Collector Editions, created to signal the end of the fifth generation and built only as needed to fill orders.

1982 Selected Colors

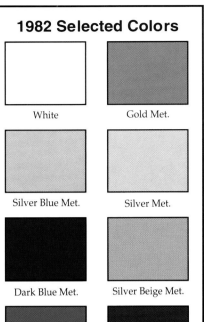

White	Gold Met.
Silver Blue Met.	Silver Met.
Dark Blue Met.	Silver Beige Met.
Bright Blue Met.	Charcoal Met.
Silver Green Met.	Spectra Red

▲ The most notable—and useful—feature of the Collector Edition was its frameless lift-up glass hatch. Base coupes stuck with a fixed rear window.

▲ All 1982 Corvettes had Turbo Hydra-matic, which added an overdrive ratio to become a four-speed unit.

▲ The Corvette logo may have evolved over the years, but it still embodied Chevrolet's creation of a racecar for the public.

▶ Four two-tone paint schemes were offered. And the modern, Kentucky plant paint shop treated each Corvette to a "clearcoat" final finish.

ENGINE SPECS

1982	L83
Type:	ohv V-8
Bore X stroke (in.):	4.00 X 3.48
Displacement (ci):	350
Compression ratio:	9.0:1
Horsepower @ rpm (bhp):	200 @ 4200
Torque @ rpm (lbs/feet):	283 @ 2800
Fuel Delivery:	Cross-Fire Throttle Body Fuel Injection
Transmission:	Turbo Hydra-Matic

DIMENSIONS

Wheelbase (in.):	98
Overall length (in.):	185.3
Overall height (in.):	48.0
Overall width (in.):	69.0
Track front/rear (in.):	58.7/59.5
Curb weight (lbs):	3495

cross-fire injection

▲ Computer Command Control electronics responded to signals from engine-mounted sensors to operate the fuel injection system. The 350-cid V-8 had 10 more horsepower than in '81.

▲ Collector Editions had silver-beige leather upholstery and door trim and a leather-wrapped steering wheel.

▼ Chevy boasted a space-age standard of fit and finish from the million-square-foot plant in Kentucky.

▲ Removable glass roof panels on the Collector Edition had solar screening. A rear defogger and power antenna were standard. A solenoid-operated hood trap door opened at full throttle, to let the Cross-Fire engine breathe easier.

1983

President Reagan called the Soviet Union "the evil empire," and opposed a nuclear arms freeze. The Strategic Defense Initiative (popularly known as the "Star Wars" program) began.

On April 18, the U.S. Embassy at Beirut was destroyed by a car bomb. In October, a bomb in a truck was driven into U.S. Marine headquarters in Lebanon, killing over 200. American forces invaded the island of Grenada that month, claiming leftists had "violently seized power."

A bipartisan commission's education report, *A Nation At Risk*, declared that American standards were "being eroded by a rising tide of mediocrity."

Sally Ride went up in the shuttle *Challenger*—the first American woman in space. Soviets shot down a Korean airliner, killing 269 people including 61 Americans. Dr. Martin Luther King's birthday was named a national holiday.

For the first time, the America's Cup left the U.S., won by Australia. Some 4.1 million VCRs were sold.

• Restyled edition expected for Corvette's 30th anniversary is delayed

• No 1983 Corvettes built; the '84 restyle won't emerge until mid-1983

• Spy shots whet enthusiasts' appetites for '84 version

• Auto production rises 10.2 percent

• GM and Toyota agree to a joint automaking venture

▲ A concept from late 1979 bears little resemblance to the Corvette.

▲ This '79 mockup put the familiar four taillights into square housings.

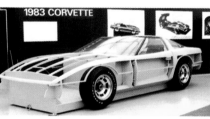

▲ By January 1980, a shop mockup was beginning to adopt final lines.

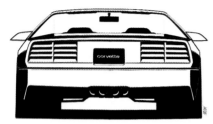

▲ This car's angular lines are more suited to Chevrolet's Camaro.

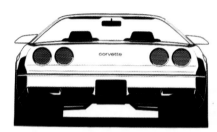

▲ This late 1979 rendition looks closer to the production sixth-generation.

▲ The final body profile was taking shape by mid-1980.

▲ Despite all the labels for a "1983 Corvette," no 30th Anniversary Edition ever materialized. Neither was a turbocharged 'Vette. Note the quarter-panel badges and the wheels.

▶ User-friendliness was a major design goal. Cockpit proposals leaned toward a space-age look, but the traditional tall center console was familiar.

1984

In July, New York became the first state to enact a compulsory seatbelt law. The Democratic Party nominated a woman to run for vice-president with Walter Mondale.

Also in July, the Olympic Games opened in Los Angeles. Soviet athletes did not attend in retaliation for the 1980 boycott against the Soviet Union.

Seventy-nine American banks failed this year—the highest figure since 1938. A Union Carbide chemical company plant leaked toxic gas in Bhopal, India.

The Reagan-Bush ticket won re-election easily on the slogan, "It's morning again in America."

New Orleans' World's Fair proved to be a financial loss. Bruce Springsteen roused fans with *Born in the U.S.A.*, and the Motion Picture Association of America created the PG-13 rating.

•First all-new Corvette in 15 years debuts, with one-piece lift-off top and lift-up rear window

•5.7-liter Cross-Fire Injection V-8 is standard, boosted slightly to 205 bhp

•Forward-opening "clamshell" hood eases servicing

•New "4+3" manual overdrive gearbox available at start of regular '84 model year

•Illuminated bar-graph instruments look futuristic, disappointing some purists

•51,547 Corvettes built, initially priced at $21,800

▲ A Turbo Corvette might have proved quite a performer, as suggested on this late '79 mockup, but the fully-restyled coupe would have the Cross-Fire V-8.

▲ Styling of the next generation began in 1975. Note the steep windshield.

▲ More notchbacked than the design at left, this one kept bulged fenders.

OVER/UNDER 1982
(INCHES)

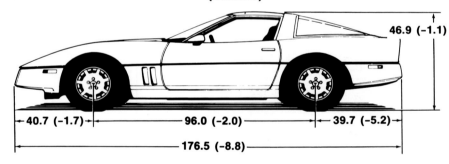

46.9 (−1.1)

40.7 (−1.7)   96.0 (−2.0)   39.7 (−5.2)

176.5 (−8.8)

OVERALL WIDTH	71.0 (+2.0)
TREAD — FRONT	59.4 (+0.7)
— REAR	60.4 (+0.9)

▲ Except for a two-inch increase in width, nearly all of the new Corvette's dimensions were smaller than in 1982 to cut weight and improve handling.

ENGINE SPECS

1984	L83
Type:	ohv V
Bore X stroke (in.):	4.00 X 3.48
Displacement (ci):	350
Compression ratio:	9.0:1
Horsepower @ rpm (bhp):	205 @ 4300
Torque @ rpm (lbs/feet):	290 @ 2800
Fuel Delivery:	Cross-Fire Throttle Body Fuel Injection
Transmission:	4-speed automatic, 4 + 3-speed manual

DIMENSIONS

Wheelbase (in.):	96.2
Overall length (in.):	176.5
Overall height (in.):	46.7
Overall width (in.):	71.0
Track front/rear (in.):	58.6/60.4
Curb weight (lbs):	3200

▲ Analog/digital speedometer and tach readouts would go into production.

▲ Gauges on this 1980 mockup would be replaced by electronics.

▲ The single-bar steering wheel would change, but instruments are close.

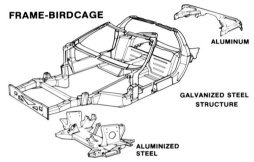

FRAME-BIRDCAGE

ALUMINUM

GALVANIZED STEEL STRUCTURE

ALUMINIZED STEEL

▲ The '84 Corvette's "birdcage" uniframe was fully welded, galvanized steel, reinforced by a bolt-on stiffening brace.

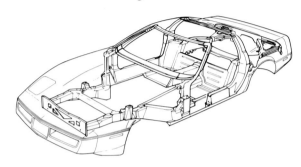

▲ "Birdcage" construction boosted Corvette safety. A bolt-on, lightweight aluminum extension supported the rear bumper.

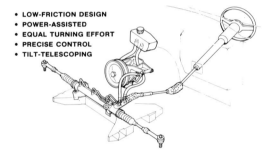

• LOW-FRICTION DESIGN
• POWER-ASSISTED
• EQUAL TURNING EFFORT
• PRECISE CONTROL
• TILT-TELESCOPING

▲ Driver-sensitive rack and pinion steering had a 15.5:1 ratio, but faster 13.0:1 gearing was available in the Z51 package.

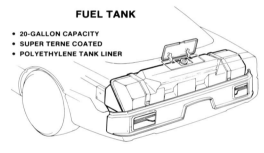

FUEL TANK

• 20-GALLON CAPACITY
• SUPER TERNE COATED
• POLYETHYLENE TANK LINER

▲ The 20-gallon fuel tank used a super terne coating to protect against corrosion and allowed long-distance cruising.

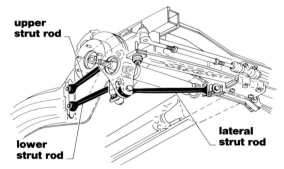

upper strut rod

lower strut rod

lateral strut rod

▲ A new five-link rear suspension used three strut rods on each side, to enhance stability and isolate noise/vibration.

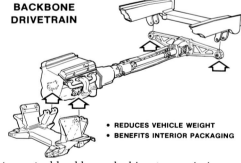

BACKBONE DRIVETRAIN

• REDUCES VEHICLE WEIGHT
• BENEFITS INTERIOR PACKAGING

▲ A Lotus-type steel backbone, lacking transmission and differential cross members, allowed more interior space.

▲ One-piece dash panel was fiberglass.

▲ In-mold coating smoothed the hood.

▲ Four parts made up the roof section.

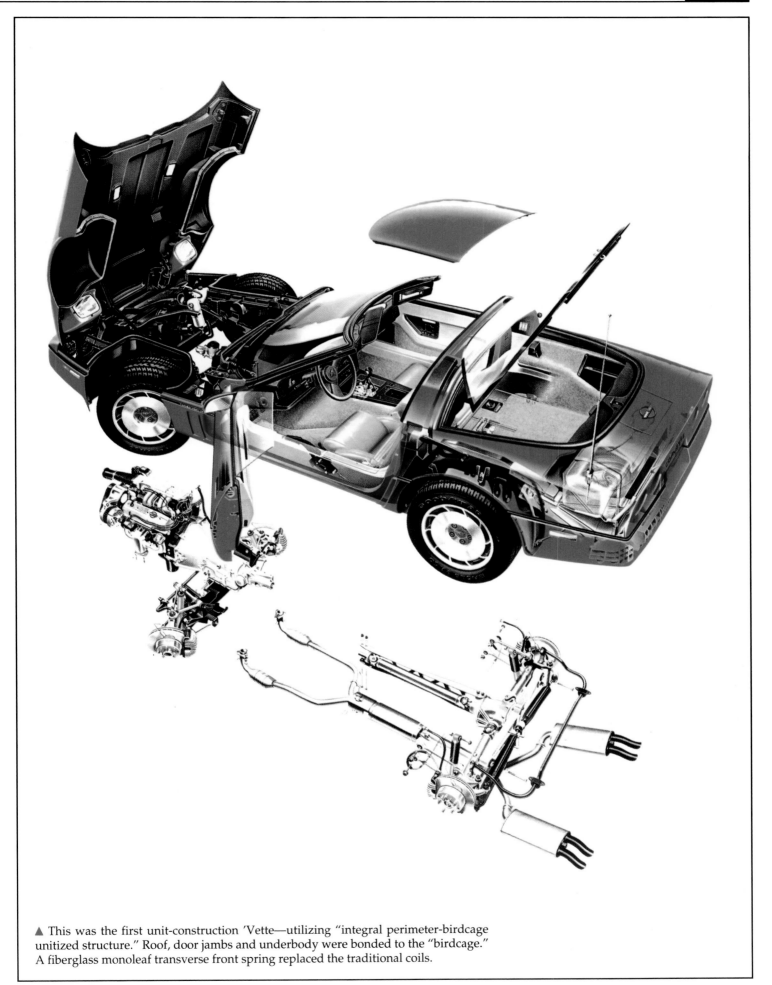

▲ This was the first unit-construction 'Vette—utilizing "integral perimeter-birdcage unitized structure." Roof, door jambs and underbody were bonded to the "birdcage." A fiberglass monoleaf transverse front spring replaced the traditional coils.

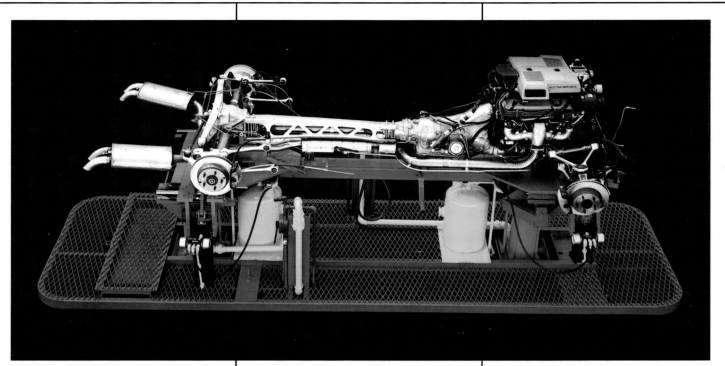

▲ The backbone drivetrain reduced weight and enhanced rigidity. An aluminum C-section "spine" connected the differential to the engine/transmission.

▶ In an effort to meet CAFE standards, a new "4+3" manual gearbox used a computer system to engage 0.67:1 overdrive ratios automatically in the top three gears, via a hydraulic clutch. An override switch soon was added.

▼ Although some of the dimensional changes were modest, proportions were definitely fresh. A wider body gave the new 'Vette its striking good looks. Door handles were more conventional.

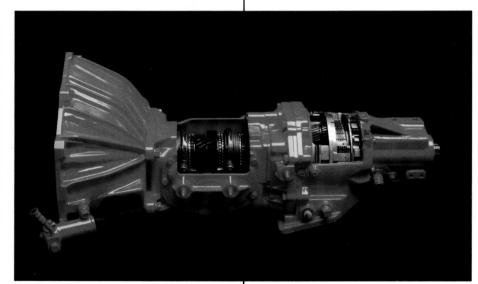

1984 Selected Colors

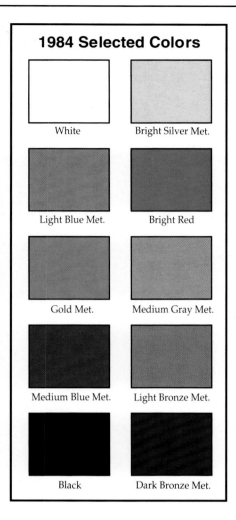

White	Bright Silver Met.
Light Blue Met.	Bright Red
Gold Met.	Medium Gray Met.
Medium Blue Met.	Light Bronze Met.
Black	Dark Bronze Met.

◄ With Cross-Fire Injection, the 5.7-liter (350-cid) V-8 developed 205 horsepower. That was only five more than before, but a 250-pound weight loss aided performance and handling.

◄ For 1985, Chevy's small-block V-8, which had been around since 1969 with 350-cid displacement, was updated with the addition of Tuned Port Fuel Injection. This replaced the imprecise Cross-Fire Injection and made the '85 'Vette a true fuelie.

▲ A perimeter rub strip completely encircled the latest Corvette, giving a more distinct upper/lower separation line and concealing the single body seam. The '84 still wore a familiar Corvette "face," even though fog and turn-signal lamps were located where air intakes had formerly dwelled.

▶ Servicing was a snap when the "clamshell" hood swung up. A cold-air induction system supplied air to the engine via a twin-duct setup. Chevy made extensive use of stainless steel and aluminum in engine and suspension parts.

▲ Overall length dropped 8.8 inches, despite only a minor cut in wheelbase (from 98.0 to 96.2 inches). The pinched-waist mid-section was gone (allowing more interior room), along with bulged fenderlines.

▲ Not everyone adored the graduated-color, 85-mph speedometer and tachometer or their matching digital readouts. Digital gauges at center included readings for range and economy.

▶ Seats were the most comfortable ever in a 'Vette, and had reclining backrests for the first time. Lear-Siegler "super seats" with inflatable lumbar adjustment cost extra.

▼ Contributing to the '84 Corvette's sleekness was its 64-degree windshield angle—steepest of any U.S. production car. Coefficient of drag dropped from 0.44 to a contemporary 0.341.

1985

On May 5, President Reagan visited a military cemetery at Bitburg, West Germany, drawing protests from Jews. In June, a TWA flight was hijacked by Arab terrorists; 39 Americans were held for 17 days.

The Supreme Court overturned an Alabama law requiring brief silent meditation at the start of each school day. A Live-Aid concert held in Philadelphia and in England raised money for African famine relief.

America now ranked as the largest debtor nation, owing $130 billion—first time a debtor since 1914. In the Soviet Union, new general secretary Mikhail Gorbachev announced sweeping reforms and a policy of perestroika.

Montgomery Ward stopped distributing mail-order catalogs after 113 years. On September 11, Pete Rose beat Ty Cobb's long-standing baseball record for career hits.

• Tuned Port Fuel Injection replaces Cross-Fire System, boosting horsepower by 25

• 5.7-liter V-8 features separate injectors for each cylinder, rates 230 bhp

• Suspension softened to improve Corvette ride

• Base price climbs to $24,873

• GTP IMSA racer debuts, sets Daytona lap record

• Improvements make Corvette a better all-around car, yet sales slump to 39,729

▲ Corvette's slippery shape—and potent new Tuned-Port fuel-injected L98 V-8 engine—provided excitement aplenty. Sticker shock had set in, however, with a starting price of $24,873. Extra-cost Lear-Siegler seats were now available in leather.

ENGINE SPECS

1985	L98
Type:	ohv V-8
Bore X stroke (in.):	4.00 X 3.48
Displacement (ci):	350
Compression ratio:	9.5:1
Horsepower @ rpm (bhp):	230 @ 4000
Torque @ rpm (lbs/feet):	330 @ 3200
Fuel Delivery:	Tuned Port Injection
Transmission:	4-speed automatic, 4 + 3-speed manual

DIMENSIONS

Wheelbase (in.):	96.2
Overall length (in.):	176.5
Overall height (in.):	46.4
Overall width (in.):	71.0
Track front/rear (in.):	59.6/60.4
Curb weight (lbs):	3230

▲ Seeking tighter quality control, the Kentucky plant used more automation. A two-stage robot welder built the uniframe.

▲ Smoothing out the body panels was still a job that required human skills to complement the ability of the machines.

▲ Unit construction made use of a perimeter "birdcage." During production, a match check frame served as an exact-size dimensional "blueprint."

▲ A combination of robots and people assured a pristine finish. A molded-in coating gave luster to fiberglass panels.

▲ The factory contained an advanced paint shop. Color was applied in a clean-room environment.

▲ Body panels got close scrutiny at each stage. The move to Kentucky was made with the sixth generation in mind.

▲ A special hydraulic "towveyer" system dropped the body onto its chassis, so each contact point matched perfectly.

▲ Exterior appearance was unchanged, except that "Tuned Port Injection" badging replaced "Cross-Fire Injection."

▶ If total restyle was the word for '84, this year's 'Vette ranked as refined. That included efforts to ease the first-year model's squeaks and rattles.

1985 Selected Colors

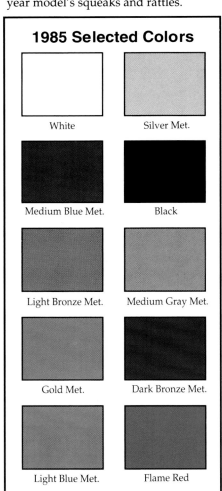

White

Silver Met.

Medium Blue Met.

Black

Light Bronze Met.

Medium Gray Met.

Gold Met.

Dark Bronze Met.

Light Blue Met.

Flame Red

▲ Multi-port fuel injection not only looked impressive, but jacked up horsepower from 205 to 230 and added 40 lbs/ft of torque. That meant quicker pickup and a top speed around 150 mph.

▲ One of the few complaints leveled against the restyled '84 Corvette was its excessively harsh ride. This year, both base and optional suspension calibrations were softened. Although the '85 was a spectacular performer and handler, some testers felt the revised suspension was still too stiff. The Z51 option now had 9.5-inch wheels all around, larger-diameter stabilizers, and gas Delco-Bilstein shocks. The manual "4+3" gearbox got a more convenient override button atop the gearshift knob and a reprogrammed computer to make it less intrusive.

▲ David McLellan, who'd succeeded Zora Arkus-Duntov as head of engineering a decade earlier, considered a Z51-equipped Corvette to be Chevrolet's "Showroom Stock GT car." Ride height dropped ¾ inch, and a revised steering caster angle gave better directional stability. An '85 could reach 60 mph in six seconds or less.

▶ A 720-horsepower, 209-cid mid-mounted, turbocharged V-6 powered this specially-constructed GTP Corvette which rode a Lola chassis. Race cars derived from this prototype were intended to compete against Porsches, Jaguars, and Ferraris in the International Motor Sports Association (IMSA) GT racing series. Chevrolet provided technical assistance for these Chevy-powered GTP cars, which ran in IMSA's Camel GT series. Only a trace of its Corvette origin is evident. Note the huge wing rear spoiler, flared ground-hugging rocker extensions, and pontoon-like rear end.

On January 28, the space shuttle *Challenger* exploded just 73 seconds after takeoff from Cape Kennedy.

In February, the U.S. recognized the new Philippine government under Corazon Aquino. On April 16, U.S. planes bombed Tripoli, Libya, in retaliation for terrorist attacks. The national debt passed the $2 trillion mark.

The Statue of Liberty marked its 100th birthday, carefully restored for the occasion. A landmark immigration bill banned the hiring of illegal aliens, but offered amnesty to all who'd been in the U.S. since 1982.

Larry McMurtry won the Pulitzer Prize for his novel *Lonesome Dove*. In the Soviet Union, the Chernobyl nuclear plant exploded near Kiev. On November 13, the Reagan administration affirmed that it had sent weapons to Iran.

- Corvette convertible is back, after 10-year absence

- Anti-lock braking debuts on Corvette—first time on an American passenger car

- Pellet-key anti-theft system added to alarm; aluminum heads arrive

- A yellow convertible, "piloted" by Chuck Yeager, serves as Indy 500 Pace Car

- All '86 convertibles sold as Pace Car replicas

- Coupe price hits $27,027; convertible lists at $32,032

- Total of 27,794 coupes and 7315 ragtops built

▲ Prices shot past $27,000 ($32,032 for the convertible), but 'Vettes had two new features: anti-lock braking and a "pass key" vehicle anti-theft system (VATS).

▲ Convertible production began by January 1986—the first since 1975. Engineered with help from the American Sunroof Company, its frame was reinforced for rigidity.

ENGINE SPECS

1986	L98
Type:	ohv V-8
Bore X stroke (in.):	4.00 X 3.48
Displacement (ci):	350
Compression ratio:	9.5:1
Horsepower @ rpm (bhp):	230 @ 4000
Torque @ rpm (lbs/feet):	330 @ 3200
Fuel Delivery:	Tuned Port Injection
Transmission:	4-speed automatic, 4 + 3-speed manual

DIMENSIONS

Wheelbase (in.):	96.2
Overall length (in.):	176.5
Overall height (in.):	47.0
Overall width (in.):	71.0
Track front/rear (in.):	59.6/60.4
Curb weight (lbs):	3101

▲ Quality control was a major goal. To create the convertible, X-braces were added and existing cowl-area K-braces stiffened.

▲ For 1986, federal law now required a high-mounted stoplamp, and the convertible's was neatly integrated into the back panel.

▲ Because the Targa-roof coupe had been redesigned for '84 with a ragtop in mind, massive chassis modification wasn't needed.

▲ Bright Yellow was an "eye-stopping" new color. The coupe's federally-ordered stoplamp rode just above the rear window.

▲ Convertible production totaled 7315, far below the 27,794 coupes. Total output dropped, largely due to high prices.

1986 Selected Colors

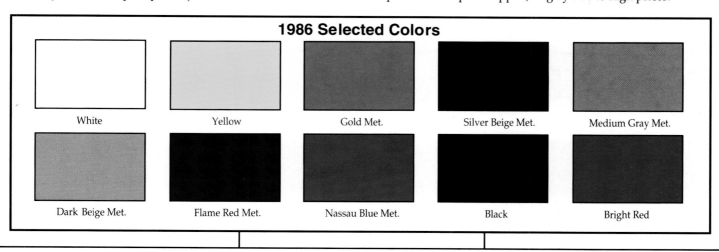

White	Yellow	Gold Met.	Silver Beige Met.	Medium Gray Met.
Dark Beige Met.	Flame Red Met.	Nassau Blue Met.	Black	Bright Red

▲ Wheels were updated this year using an unidirectional design, and convertibles were identical to the one that paced the Indianapolis 500-mile race this year, except for the pace car's special lighting and strobed lamps.

▶ Re-angled instruments were easier to see in daylight, and a new upshift indicator light was installed even on automatic-transmission cars. The convertible top folded manually, hidden beneath a spring-loaded lift-up cover.

▲ A resistor pellet mounted in the ignition key had to be "read" by a hidden decoder before the engine would start. If no pellet or the wrong key was used, the ignition would be disabled for two minutes, effectively thwarting would-be car thieves.

▶ Beneath the hood sat the familiar 5.7-liter L98 V-8 with Tuned Port Injection, still rated 230 bhp. By mid-year, weight-saving aluminum heads were installed to replace cast iron. They had central copper-core spark plugs, larger intake ports, and sintered-metal valve seats. A revised exhaust system used triple catalytic converters.

▲ Since all 1986 ragtops were considered Indy Pace Car Replicas, each included decals. Not every owner chose to use them. Convertible suspensions were stiffer than base coupes.

▲ Chevrolet continued to call its convertible a "roadster," advertising that the '86 pace car was the latest of seven Chevrolets to receive that honor since 1948.

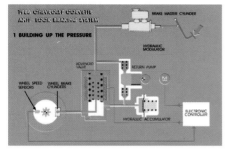

▲ Anti-lock braking sensors detected speed of each wheel and signaled controller to ease pressure as lock-up neared.

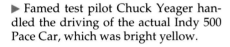

▶ Famed test pilot Chuck Yeager handled the driving of the actual Indy 500 Pace Car, which was bright yellow.

◀ The 1986 version of the Corvette-derived GTP racer ran in the IMSA Camel GT series, winning twice and taking seven pole positions. Note the tall, adjustable wing spoiler.

1986 Corvette Indy

Late in 1985, Chevrolet showcased a street version of its Indy-car V-8 engine in a futuristic mid-engine concept car called the Corvette Indy. Its Ilmor 2.65-liter V-8 held twin intercooled turbos. Less than a year later came a driveable prototype, with a 5.7-liter, 32-valve V-8, which many felt would shape the next Corvette. Features included "active" suspension and ETAK navigation, plus provisions for "drive-by-wire" controls to replace the throttle.

▲ Development of the wildly styled, mid-engine Indy took its cues from the earlier Aerovette and XP-895. As this rendering suggests, GM sought a voluptuous, low-slung shape for its design project, per the theme of styling chief Irwin Rybicki.

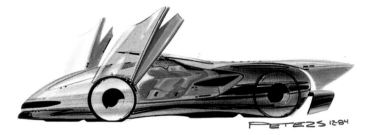
▲ Scissor-hinged doors in this rendering would be part of the Indy concept but, add-on ground effects would not be seen.

▲ This huggable-looking study roughly captures the basic Indy shape, but the glassed cockpit would move farther forward.

▲ Though fanciful, renderings like this helped stylists develop the Indy's rounded stub nose and cab-forward profile.

▲ This March 1985 creation with wild rear end makes it clear that stylists were encouraged to push current design limits.

▲ Though designed around the Ilmor engine that dominated the CART Indy-car series, the Indy unveiled in late 1985 was inoperative. Its reverse-curve rear held a low "loop" spoiler.

▲ The Corvette Indy concept car appears to be in good company at this event, sitting next to a Ferrari. Huge, forward-facing air scoops cut deep into lower bodysides.

▲ The Indy's smooth bubble canopy pushed forward toward a rounded, ground-sniffing nose and had a small removable center section.

▶ With a rear end designed for peak downforce, the Indy was intended to accept 4WD and four-wheel steering.

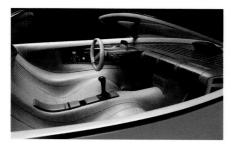

▲ A soft-contour dash held twin video screens and plenty of pushbuttons.

▲ Whereas the first Indy had used a Kevlar tub, this running prototype rode a backbone chassis of carbon fiber. "Active Suspension" provided quick responses to changing conditions.

▲ The Indy's LT5 aluminum 5.7-liter V-8, with twin-cam heads and 16 tuned intake runners, previewed the engine that would power the Corvette ZR-1. Note the multi-LED taillamp.

1987

On March 18, Congress voted to raise the speed limit on rural highways to 65 mph. News reports from Los Angeles noted that freeway motorists were firing guns at other drivers.

On March 19, TV evangelist Jim Bakker resigned his ministry in a sex scandal. In July, Colonel Oliver North testified before a Senate and House committee on his role in the Iran-Contra affair. On October 19, the stock market dropped 508 points in its worst day ever. Four days later, Robert Bork's nomination to the Supreme Court was rejected. Meanwhile, U.S. Navy warships shelled an Iranian oil platform in retaliation for an attack on an American tanker.

In February, the yacht *Liberty* regained the America's Cup, defeating an Australian entry. Top films included *Platoon*, *Wall Street*, and *The Last Emperor*.

- Corvette is largely a carryover

- New roller valve lifters boost output of 5.7-liter V-8 engine to 240 horsepower

- Six-way power passenger's seat joins option list

- Major components get ID marks to thwart thieves

- Production of 30,632 Corvettes includes 10,625 convertibles, 20,007 coupes

- Coupe lists for $27,999, ragtop for $33,172

- Corvettes undefeated in SCCA stock racing for fourth year in a row

▲ Modest changes took place under the hood for 1987. New roller-type valve lifters reduced frictional losses. Rocker arm covers received raised rails to forestall oil leaks, and spark plugs moved closer to the center of each combustion chamber.

ENGINE SPECS	
1987	L98
Type:	ohv V-8
Bore X stroke (in.):	4.00 X 3.48
Displacement (ci):	350
Compression ratio:	9.5:1
Horsepower @ rpm (bhp):	240 @ 4000
Torque @ rpm (lbs/feet):	345 @ 3200
Fuel Delivery:	Tuned Port Injection
Transmission:	4-speed automatic, 4 + 3-speed manual

DIMENSIONS	
Wheelbase (in.):	96.2
Overall length (in.):	176.5.3
Overall height (in.):	48.0
Overall width (in.):	69.0
Track front/rear (in.):	58.7/59.5
Curb weight (lbs):	3216

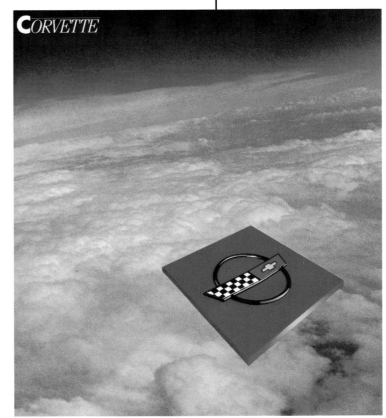

▲ Horsepower of the 5.7-liter V-8 rose by 10 (to 240), and torque twisted upward again to a stump-pulling 345 lbs/ft. An optional six-way power passenger's seat matched the driver's. Many major parts got ID marks to foil thieves.

▲ Hidden headlights still were part of the Corvette mystique. Yet sales continued their downward trend, with 30,632 built, but the ragtop gained about 3300.

◀ A new Z52 suspension option for the coupe, at $470, was a softer version of the Z51 package with wider (9.5-inch) wheels, solid (thicker) front anti-roll bar, gas-charged shocks, quick-ratio steering, and chassis stiffening.

1987 Selected Colors

White	Silver Met.
Yellow	Gold Met.
Medium Gray Met.	Silver Beige Met.
Dark Red Met.	Black
Bright Red	Medium Brown Met.

▲ Callaway Engineering created the Twin-Turbo—officially a $19,000 Corvette option. The engine made 345 horsepower, and a stump-pulling 465 lbs/ft of torque.

▲ Anti-lock braking was standard—a sensible feature for a car that could top 150 mph. The anti-theft system disabled the starter and fuel pump if tampering was detected. A tire-pressure monitor had been announced, but would be delayed.

▼ With manual shift, an '87 could shoot to 60 mph in 6.3 seconds. A race-oriented Z51 option listed at $795, but its super-stiff springs could produce pain in ordinary driving. It wasn't even offered with automatic or on convertibles.

◄ The Corvette Geneve was built on a stock chassis by ASC Inc. of Southgate, Michigan, to demonstrate "how advanced design elements can be integrated with pure practicality." Noticeably absent was the full body molding as well as the use of a new wheel design.

▼ Geneve styling was reminiscent of the Indy—notably the low, gently curved nose and dished hood. Race-inspired rocker-panel skirts swept around the nose and tail, while door handles blended neatly into body moldings.

▲ Blending the look of the fifth and sixth generations, the Geneve wore twin rear spoilers—one below the tail plus a well-integrated "winglet" above. A high-mount stoplamp using high-intensity LEDs was neatly installed in the upper spoiler.

▲ Identification of the ASC Corvette was easy enough—just peek inside to see "Geneve" stitched in bright red on upper seat backrests. Lower portions of the "sculptured" seats, wearing charcoal suede inserts, had a pleasingly plush look. The cockpit was similar to stock, but used plenty of black leather.

In April, Soviets agreed to withdraw troops from Pakistan and Afghanistan. After Mikhail Gorbachev's confirmation as president, they initiated an era of *glasnost* (openness) and *perestroika* (restructuring).

A UN cease-fire ended the Iran-Iraq war after a U.S. ship had inadvertently shot down an Iranian airliner with 290 aboard.

George Bush easily won the presidency over Massachusetts governor Michael Dukakis, taking 40 states. Bush's vice-presidential choice was Indiana senator J. Danforth Quayle.

After a dry summer, Yellowstone National Park was besieged by a dozen fires.

The B-2 (Stealth) bomber was unveiled, said to be virtually invisible to radar. Pan Am flight 103 crashed at Lockerbie, Scotland.

• Corvette unchanged except for engine/chassis upgrades

• "35th Anniversary" Corvette sports white body and white leather interior

• Tuned Port Injection V-8 produces 245 bhp, with freer-breathing cylinder heads

• 17-inch wheels and tires join the option list

• 50 identical Corvettes compete in "Corvette Challenge," sponsored by Sports Car Club of America

• Coupe lists for $29,480, ragtop for $34,820

• Output slips to 22,789

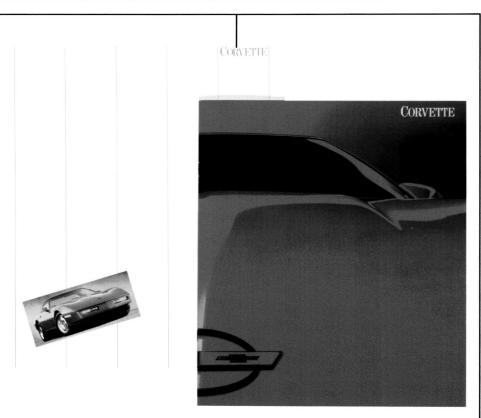

▲ For its 35th year, Corvette earned some engine and chassis improvements. An anniversary edition bowed at the New York Auto Show, with only 2000 to be built.

▲ The suspension was modified and the V-8 upped to 245 bhp, via freer-breathing heads and a reprofiled cam.

▼ The familiar fold-down, left-side parking brake lever moved lower and back. Leather sport seats cost $1025.

ENGINE SPECS

1988	L98
Type:	ohv V-8
Bore X stroke (in.):	4.00 X 3.48
Displacement (ci):	350
Compression ratio:	9.5:1
Horsepower @ rpm (bhp):	245[1] @ 4300
Torque @ rpm (lbs/feet):	340 @ 3200
Fuel Delivery:	Tuned Port Injection
Transmission:	4-speed automatic,
	4 + 3-speed manual

[1]240 bhp on convertibles and coupes with a 2.59:1 real axle.

DIMENSIONS

Wheelbase (in.):	96.2
Overall length (in.):	175.3
Overall height (in.):	46.7
Overall width (in.):	71.0
Track front/rear (in.):	59.6/60.4
Curb weight (lbs):	3233

▲ Customers could order huge P275/40ZR17 Z-rated tires separately or as part of the $1295 Z51 handling package. Front suspension geometry was reworked for better directional control in hard stops, while the rear offered tighter stability.

▲ Standard 16-inch wheels got new styling and Z-rated P245/60VR16 Eagle rubber (good for 149+ mph). Blue or bronze lift-off roof panels cost $615.

▲ Brakes gained thicker rotors, plus a handbrake integrated with the rear disc brakes. A "4+3" overdrive manual or four-speed automatic transmission could be ordered.

◀ Styling showed no evident change. Automatic temperature control had been phased in as an option during 1987.

▼ With Corvette barred from Showroom Stock racing after '87, Chevy and SCCA formed a Corvette Challenge Series.

▲ A mid-engine prototype for IMSA's Camel GT series, supported by Chevy, was built around a long-tail monocoque of Kevlar and aluminum honeycomb.

▶ Here, GM's "Goodwrench" car, with chassis engineered by Lola of England, ran under the auspices of the Hendrick Motorsports race team.

▲ A turbo-intercooled 90-degree V-6 in the GTP used many off-the-shelf parts but developed 775 bhp at 8500 rpm. Note the vast rear wing on slim struts.

▲ The striking 35th Anniversary coupe, option Z01, had a bright white lower body (including color-matched handles, mirrors, moldings and 17-inch wheels), with black roof hoop and transparent black acrylic panel. Special badges went around front-fender "gills," and as embroidery on seatbacks in the white leather interior.

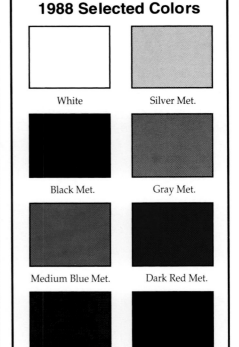

1988 Selected Colors

White	Silver Met.
Black Met.	Gray Met.
Medium Blue Met.	Dark Red Met.
Dark Smoke Gray Met.	Black

1989

On March 24, the tanker *Exxon Valdez* ran aground in Alaska, sending more than 10 million gallons of crude oil into the sea—the worst oil spill in American history.

Student protests in China culminated in the Tiananmen Square massacre in Beijing in June.

President Bush signed a bill authorizing relief for savings and loan institutions. *Batman* was among the major movies of the year.

Charleston, South Carolina, was hit hard by Hurricane Hugo in September. An earthquake struck San Francisco on October 17, registering 6.9 on the Richter scale. Dozens of people were killed.

To the amazement of people around the world, Eastern European Communist governments began to fall. The Berlin Wall came down on November 9, ending the long-lived "iron curtain."

• Total of 26,412 Corvettes built in 1989 model year

• Removable hardtop for convertible returns with heated back window

• 17-inch aluminum wheels and unidirectional tires become standard equipment

• Low-tire-pressure warning system available

• ZF six-speed manual gearbox becomes standard, with computer-aided 1-4 shift during light acceleration

• Delco-Bilstein Selective Ride Control optional

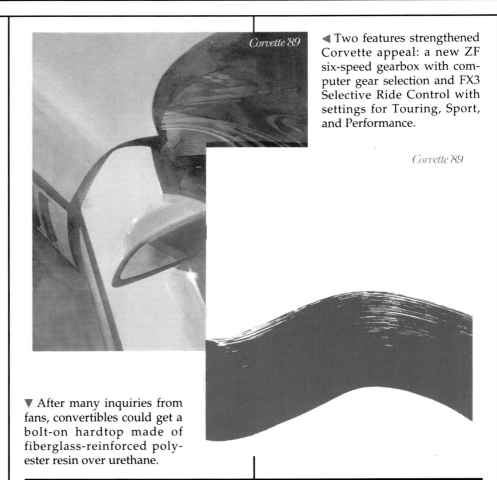

Corvette '89

◄ Two features strengthened Corvette appeal: a new ZF six-speed gearbox with computer gear selection and FX3 Selective Ride Control with settings for Touring, Sport, and Performance.

Corvette '89

▼ After many inquiries from fans, convertibles could get a bolt-on hardtop made of fiberglass-reinforced polyester resin over urethane.

▲ The removable hardtop had single-bolt attachment, and included a cloth headliner and heated rear window.

▲ ASC Inc. helped engineer the new hardtop. Molded around a steel/aluminum "cage" and given a protective coating, it gave the convertible the look of a notchback.

▲ Base price of this year's coupe was $31,545. The new tri-mode suspension came only on coupes with a manual gearbox and Z51 handling package.

◄ A convertible listed at $36,785, with much of the former Z52 suspension now standard. New optional leather sport seats had full lumbar adjustment.

▲ All 'Vettes had fast-ratio steering, 17-inch tires, Delco/Bilstein gas shocks, and a fortified front-end.

▲ Announced two years earlier, an optional electronic tire-pressure monitoring system was now available.

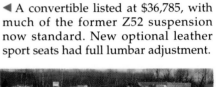

▲ Cars with a six-speed had the Z51 option's engine oil cooler, heavy-duty radiator, and auxiliary radiator fan.

▲ The $1995 removable hardtop could fit any sixth-generation convertible.

1989 Selected Colors

White	Medium Blue Met.
Dark Blue Met.	Black
Dark Red Met.	Bright Red

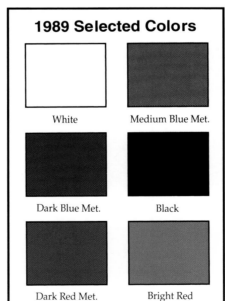

▲ Dashboard of ZR-1 had analog and digital displays instead of all digital.

▲ The ZR-1 was announced late in 1988. However, only the standard L98 engine actually emerged in '89, unchanged except for new Multec fuel injectors from ZR-1.

▲ Though anticipated as a 1989 model, only a handful of ZR-1s were built before the '90 model year. Viewed from the side, they differed from regular coupes mainly in the convex rear end. A major goal of the ZR-1 program was to mix breathtaking performance with "a pussycat personality."

▶ Chevrolet issued a specific set of demands for the ZR-1 engine, which was developed by Lotus and produced Mercury Marine. Power and torque would have to be 50 percent greater than the base engine, with overall economy of at least 22.5 mpg.

▼ External size of the ZR-1 engine had to be compatible with the existing Corvette body/chassis structure. Aimed at satisfying the most demanding enthusiasts, the supercar soon acquired the nickname "King of the Hill" from the press.

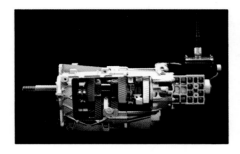

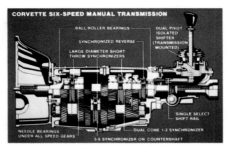

To help meet mileage standards, the new six-speed was computer-controlled to shift from first gear to fourth when light throttle openings were indicated.

Alongside a regular Corvette, a ZR-1 was a wolf amongst sheep. Rear fenders had to bulge to accept wider tires.

A procession of early ZR-1s was easy to spot by their square taillights in a wide, convex-shaped rear end.

Super-powered ZR-1s were assembled alongside L98 Corvettes, but their Lotus-designed aluminum V-8s, with four valves per cylinder, came from a Mercury Marine plant in Oklahoma.

The "LT5" designation had been used in 1986 on the Indy show car's engine, which previewed the 375-horsepower, four-cam V-8 that went into the ZR-1.

ENGINE SPECS

1989	L98	LT5
Type:	ohv V-8	dohc V-8
Bore X stroke (in.):	4.00 X 3.48	3.90 X 3.66
Displacement (ci):	350	350
Compression ratio:	9.5:1	11.25:1
Horsepower @ rpm (bhp):	245 @ 4300	375 @ 5800
Torque @ rpm (lbs/feet):	340 @ 3200	370 @ 4800
Fuel Delivery:	Tuned Port Injection	Tuned Port Injection
Transmission:	4-speed automatic, 6-speed manual	6-speed manual

DIMENSIONS

Wheelbase (in.):	96.2
Overall length (in.):	175.3 (177.4 ZR-1)
Overall height (in.):	46.7
Overall width (in.):	71.0 (74.0 ZR-1)
Track front/rear (in.):	59.6/60.4 (61.9 ZR-1)
Curb weight (lbs):	3233 (3465 ZR-1)

1990

On January 3, Panamanian General Manuel Noriega surrendered to U.S. military forces following an invasion of Panama. South Africa lifted its ban on the African National Congress on February 2, then released black leader Nelson Mandela after more than 27 years in prison.

Iraqi troops crossed into Kuwait on August 2. Iraqi president Saddam Hussein soon announced annexation of that country as Kuwait's ruling family fled into exile. The United Nations then imposed economic sanctions against Iraq, and U.S. forces began a military buildup in the area.

East and West Germany were reunified on October 3, and leaders of 34 nations signed the Charter of Paris, ending the Cold War. Lech Walesa became president of Poland.

"Junk bond king" Michael Milken was sentenced to 10 years in prison. Warren Beatty and Madonna starred in the movie *Dick Tracy*.

- Driver-side air bag becomes 'Vette standard

- Restyled wraparound instrument panel holds analog and digital displays

- Eagerly awaited ZR-1 on sale, for a whopping $58,995; total of 3049 built

- All-aluminum 32-valve, dual-overhead-cam LT5 V-8 in ZR-1 develops 375 bhp

- Wider convex ZR-1 rear end wears rectangular taillights

▲ All Corvettes received a new dash that was much more jet fighter-like and mixed digital and analog gauges. Also new was a redesigned steering wheel with an air bag. Seats and console were reworked. The ZR-1 (shown) included standard FX3 Selective Ride Control and low-tire-pressure warning.

▲ Developed by Lotus and produced by Mercury Marine, the ZR-1's mighty four-cam aluminum V-8 yielded 375 bhp. On March 2, a ZR-1 prepared by Tommy Morrison Motorsports smashed the land-speed record established by Ab Jenkins nearly a half-century earlier, traveling 24 hours at an average speed of 175.885 mph.

1990 Selected Colors

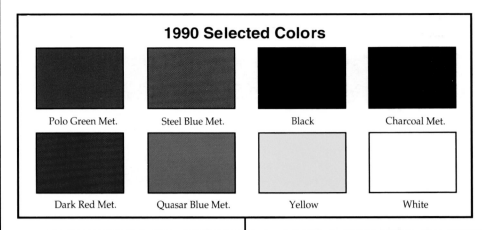

| Polo Green Met. | Steel Blue Met. | Black | Charcoal Met. |
| Dark Red Met. | Quasar Blue Met. | Yellow | White |

▼ Like previous Corvettes, the fiberglass body of the present generation allows easy customization. Larry Shinoda, mastermind behind designs such as the '63 split-window coupe, teamed with racecar driver Rick Mears to create the Rick Mears Special Edition Package. Shinoda stands between a '90 Corvette fitted with the package and a split-window coupe.

▲ The 10-piece package attached directly to any '84 or later Corvette. This 1986 model shows off the lower body treatment with silver painted body panels. Front lights, fasteners, and primed semi-rigid polyurethane panels are included in each kit.

▲ A total of 3049 customers had an opportunity to pay $58,995 ($27,016 above the base coupe) for a blast of exuberant ZR-1 force—and a chance to show neighbors that they owned one of the hottest machines ever to hit the pavement.

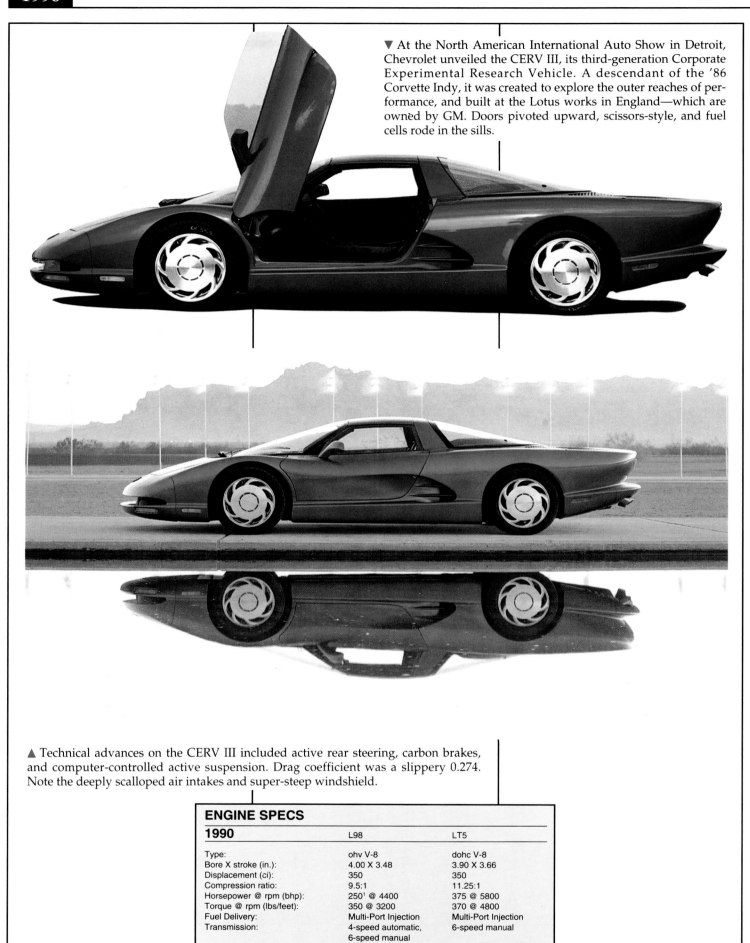

▼ At the North American International Auto Show in Detroit, Chevrolet unveiled the CERV III, its third-generation Corporate Experimental Research Vehicle. A descendant of the '86 Corvette Indy, it was created to explore the outer reaches of performance, and built at the Lotus works in England—which are owned by GM. Doors pivoted upward, scissors-style, and fuel cells rode in the sills.

▲ Technical advances on the CERV III included active rear steering, carbon brakes, and computer-controlled active suspension. Drag coefficient was a slippery 0.274. Note the deeply scalloped air intakes and super-steep windshield.

ENGINE SPECS

1990	L98	LT5
Type:	ohv V-8	dohc V-8
Bore X stroke (in.):	4.00 X 3.48	3.90 X 3.66
Displacement (ci):	350	350
Compression ratio:	9.5:1	11.25:1
Horsepower @ rpm (bhp):	250[1] @ 4400	375 @ 5800
Torque @ rpm (lbs/feet):	350 @ 3200	370 @ 4800
Fuel Delivery:	Multi-Port Injection	Multi-Port Injection
Transmission:	4-speed automatic, 6-speed manual	6-speed manual

[1]245 bhp on convertibles and coupes with a 2.59:1 real axle.

DIMENSIONS

Wheelbase (in.):	96.2
Overall length (in.):	176.3 (177.4 ZR-1)
Overall height (in.):	46.7
Overall width (in.):	71.0 (74.0 ZR-1)
Track front/rear (in.):	59.6/60.4 (61.9 ZR-1)
Curb weight (lbs):	3233 (3465 ZR-1)

▲ Twin video displays and a panorama of analog gauges displayed all vital data to a potential CERV III driver. Readouts included diagnostics, active-suspension parameters, and 4WD torque split.

▲ A twin-turbo 5.7-liter, 32-valve V-8, based on the ZR-1's, lurked behind the CERV III cockpit—boasting about 650 bhp. Three-speed Turbo Hydra-Matic sat in series with a two-speed gearbox giving six forward gears.

▲ Manager of the CERV III project was Richard L. Balsley of Advanced Vehicle Engineering. The team's goal: top performance in a car that was "predictable," able to "forgive" driver error. Chevy denied that the CERV III foretold a future 'Vette.

1991

On January 16, less than a day after a UN deadline for Iraqi withdrawal from Kuwait, Allied air attacks against Iraqi forces began. Saddam Hussein retaliated by firing Scud missiles at Israeli cities. A cease-fire was announced at the end of February, four days after the beginning of a smashingly successful Allied land campaign.

On August 21, a right-wing-coup attempt against Soviet president Gorbachev collapsed after two days. On Christmas Day, Gorbachev resigned and the USSR was disbanded.

Millions watched on TV as Supreme Court nominee Clarence Thomas countered charges of sexual harassment by professor Anita Hill. On December 4, Terry Anderson, the last U.S. hostage in Lebanon, was released. Unemployment by year's end hit 7.1 percent.

The Chicago Bulls won their first National Basketball Association championship.

- Corvette earns its first facelift since 1984

- Regular models wear rectangular taillights and convex rear from ZR-1

- Styling features also include horizontal front fender louvers, wraparound front cornering lamps

- Coupe lists for $32,455, ragtop for $38,770; ZR-1 coupe comes to $64,138

- 17-inch wheels restyled

- Output slips to 20,639

▲ The first Corvette facelift since 1984 included a smooth, tapered, lower nose with wraparound cornering/parking lamps. At the cowl, four horizontal strakes replaced the former twin vertical gills. Bodyside moldings were body-colored, wheels restyled, and convertibles could get the optional FX3 Selective Ride Control.

▲ New mufflers with lower back-pressure didn't affect the output of the L98 engine. The convertible started at $38,770, the coupe at $32,455. Buying a ZR-1 supercoupe took an extra $31,683. This year's owners didn't get so unique a product, however, as all 'Vettes adopted ZR-1 styling touches. Flicking the "valet" key slashed the ZR-1's output to a mere 210 horses.

ENGINE SPECS

1991	L98	LT5
Type:	ohv V-8	dohc V-8
Bore X stroke (in.):	4.00 X 3.48	3.90 X 3.66
Displacement (ci):	350	350
Compression ratio:	10.0:1	11.0:1
Horsepower @ rpm (bhp):	250 @ 4400	375 @ 5800
Torque @ rpm (lbs/feet):	350 @ 3200	370 @ 4800
Fuel Delivery:	Multi-Port Injection	Multi-Port Injection
Transmission:	4-speed automatic, 6-speed manual	6-speed manual

DIMENSIONS

Wheelbase (in.):	96.2
Overall length (in.):	178.6 (178.5 ZR-1)
Overall height (in.):	46.7
Overall width (in.):	71.0 (73.2 ZR-1)
Track front/rear (in.):	59.6/60.4 (61.9 ZR-1)
Curb weight (lbs):	3294 (3470 ZR-1)

◀ Interiors changed little except for the addition of an auxiliary 12-volt power plug, and a "delay" feature that delivered power to the stereo and power windows for up to 15 minutes after ignition switch-off. A standard power-steering fluid cooler became standard. Leather seats added $1050, while the FX3 suspension cost $1695.

▲ A quieter exhaust note was the only noticeable change for the L98 engine, which developed 250 horsepower.

▶ All Corvettes now sported ZR-1's convex tail and square lights. The coupe and convertible's stoplamps were moved to the back panel, while the ZR-1's stayed above the backlight.

▼ A new Z07 high-performance suspension melded the tri-mode FX3 and stiff Z51. An L98 could hit 60 in 5.3 seconds.

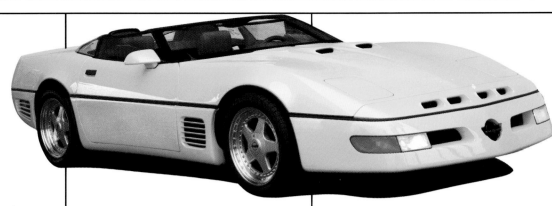

▶ Callaway Engineering debuted a new aero-bodied Twin-Turbo Corvette Speedster at the Los Angeles Auto Show. This Pearl Yellow example is one of 10 built, styled with fixed side windows.

▲ Powering the Callaway Speedster: a 450-bhp version of the Corvette 5.7-liter TPI V-8 (600 lbs/ft of torque), with six-speed gearbox. Also included were O.Z. brand racing wheels.

▲ The Callaway Speedster's cut-down windshield wrapped the A-pillars, extending to headrests. The open-top design aimed at Californians; custom interiors wore Connolly leather.

▲ An ultra-low profile and long, tunneled rear window gave the Callaway Speedster a distinctive aura. Various styling touches, including fender louvers and four-slot nose, evolved from earlier "Sledgehammer," but hood scoops were new. Callaway first expected to build 50, and then no more. Prices started at $107,000.

1991 Selected Colors

Arctic White	Turquoise Met.
Medium Quasar Blue Met.	Dark Polo Green Met.
Steel Blue Met.	Competition Yellow
Bright Red	Dark Smoke Gray Met.

▲ Tinkering with Corvettes was a popular pastime with aftermarket companies and GM execs. Here, Executive Director of GM Design Jerry Palmer stands behind his "Mean Machine" convertible.

▲ "Mean Machine" styling wasn't much different from production Corvettes except for wheels, but the wild pinkish-purple paint made it quite a standout. Advanced Vehicle Engineering head Don Runkle got a specially-built ZR-1 Spyder, styled like early '60s roadsters, with a top boot that extended into the passenger section.

The Postal Service created a contest to select a stamp to honor Elvis Presley. On February 27, General Motors announced a $4.45 billion loss for 1991, warning of layoffs and plant closings. GM chairman Robert Stempel, under pressure from the GM board of directors, resigned in October. Chief Corvette design engineer David McLellan opted for early retirement.

Arkansas governor Bill Clinton and Tennessee Senator Albert Gore defeated George Bush and Dan Quayle, placing a Democrat in the White House for the first time since 1980. Multi-billionaire Texas businessman H. Ross Perot garnered almost 20% of the vote.

Rioting began in Los Angeles on April 29, after four white policemen were acquitted of beating black motorist Rodney King. Hurricane Andrew struck south Florida with a fury on August 14, leaving a quarter-million homeless.

•Second-generation, LT1 small-block 5.7-liter V-8 debuts with 300 bhp

•Bosch Acceleration Slip Regulation (traction control) and new Goodyear tires enhance Corvette's all-weather capability

•Millionth Corvette is a white convertible with red interior, like the first two-seater in 1953; goes to National Corvette Museum

•Total of 20,479 Corvettes built in model year

▲ Acceleration Slip Regulation (traction control) helped give Corvettes an all-weather image, eliminating their frightful twitchiness on wet pavement. A dash button allowed the ASR to be disabled. The new LT1 engine, reviving a designation used in 1970-72, made 50 more horsepower (300) than the L98, though torque dipped a bit.

▲ Two rectangular exhaust tips were used instead of four. Asymmetrical-tread Eagle GS-C tires replaced the Gatorbacks, making each tire specific to that corner of the car. Bosch created the standard traction control, which cut engine power (or applied brakes) as soon as a wheel began to slip.

▲ With the more potent LT1 V-8, the standard Corvette's blast-off performance began to rival that of the ZR-1 supercar. This was the highest net horsepower for a small-block in Chevrolet history. This year's convertible started at $40,145 (almost double the $21,000 price of the '84 base model).

▲ Dashboards received all-black look and soft-touch feel. Though ZR-1 sales fell short of expectations, the car survived the corporate axe.

▲ Once again, a ZR-1 had 375 horses and 370 lbs/ft of torque to play with.

▶ Little marked a ZR-1 except its new badges—and the lush sound of its V-8.

▼ Actual selling prices for the ZR-1 fell below its $65,318 list figure.

▲ On July 2, 1992 (a bit earlier than expected), the one-millionth Corvette rolled off the line at Bowling Green.

▲ In late 1992, David C. Hill became only the third chief engineer for the Corvette, succeeding David McLellan and Zora Arkus-Duntov.

1992 Selected Colors

Arctic White Solid	Black
Bright Aqua Met.	Medium Green Met.
Yellow Solid	Dark Green Gray Met.

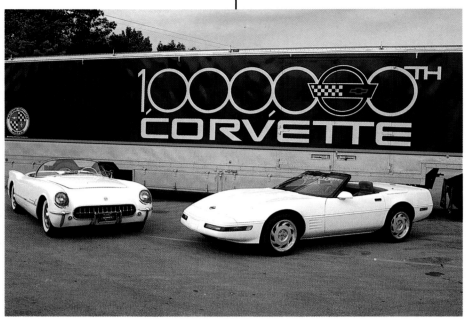

▲ Both the one-millionth Corvette and the original '53 were white convertibles with red interiors. Chevrolet chief Jim Perkins called the 'Vette "an American institution." Groundbreaking for the new Corvette museum near Bowling Green came in June.

▲ Some major figures in Corvette history showed up to see the one-millionth car. Former chief engineer David McLellan stands at left (in shirtsleeves). Zora Arkus-Duntov, his predecessor, is at driver's door, ahead of Chevy general manager Jim Perkins.

DIMENSIONS

Wheelbase (in.):	96.2
Overall length (in.):	178.5
Overall height (in.):	46.3 (47.3 ZR-1)
Overall width (in.):	70.7 (73.1 ZR-1)
Track front/rear (in.):	57.7/59.1 (60.6 ZR-1)
Curb weight (lbs):	3327 (3415 ZR-1)

ENGINE SPECS

1992	LT1	LT5
Type:	ohv V-8	dohc V-8
Bore X stroke (in.):	4.00 X 3.48	3.90 X 3.66
Displacement (ci):	350	350
Compression ratio:	10.5:1	11.0:1
Horsepower @ rpm (bhp):	300 @ 5000	375 @ 5800
Torque @ rpm (lbs/feet):	330 @ 4000	370 @ 4800
Fuel Delivery:	Multi-Port Injection	Multi-Port Injection
Transmission:	4-speed automatic, 6-speed manual	6-speed manual

▲ The Corvette Challenge Series ended after '89, when 'Vettes became eligible for a new SCCA World Challenge. Corvette took that championship in 1990 and '91.

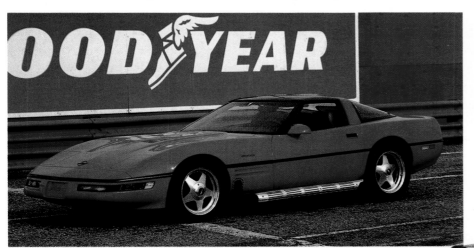

▲ Stuffed under the hood of this tough coupe is a V-12 monster with 650 bhp.

◄ Except for side exhaust and ZR-12 badge, V-12 'Vette looks nearly stock.

▲ To accept the V-12, the wheelbase of the Corvette had to be stretched by eight inches, with a longer hood installed.

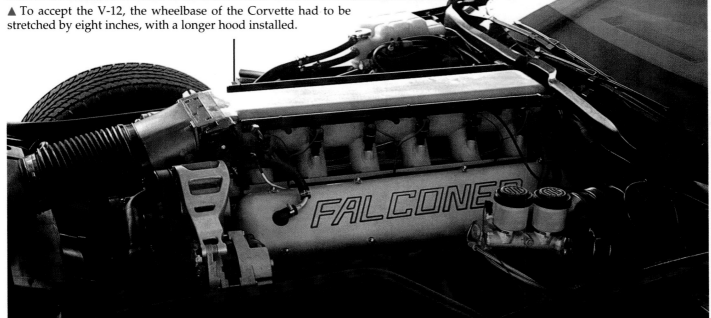

▲ Ryan Falconer of Salinas, California, developed the aluminum V-12, based on the Corvette small-block. Only one car was built at the request of GM engineers. Earlier, Chevrolet folks had stuffed a 454-cid big-block into a one-off ZR2.

1993

The Cold War was history, but many Americans wondered as 1993 began whether a real economic recovery would ever come to pass.

Chevrolet, on a far more positive note, celebrated the 40th anniversary of its two-seat sports car. The Corvette had come a long way from its beginning as one of the first fiberglass-bodied vehicles to go into serious production. The first six-cylinder engine, hooked to relatively anemic Powerglide, had quickly evolved into a long series of potent powerhouse V-8s. At the same time, the handling and roadability of America's only true sports car kept getting better.

Corvette survived its feared demise in the late 1950s, and also survived the detuning of the 1970s as new emissions and safety standards emerged. Today, it's a living legend that continues to attract a loyal following of customers.

• Corvette marks its 40th year of production

• 40th anniversary option package offered on all Corvette models, including convertible and ZR-1

• ZR-1 engine adds 30 horsepower, reaching an astounding 405 bhp

• Regular Corvettes get ride/handling improvements including narrower front wheels and tires

• Passive Keyless Entry locks and unlocks door as driver approaches and departs

▲ America's only true production sports car got slightly narrower front wheels, adding managability.

▲ All Corvettes added a Passive Keyless Entry system. Approach the car and the doors unlocked automatically—no action needed.

▲ Ratings of the LT1 engine were the same as '92: 300 bhp at 5000 rpm. A safeguard in the Keyless Entry system prevented locking keys inside the car.

▲ Starting in '93, no more than 380 ZR-1s would go on sale per year. General manager Jim Perkins called ZR-1 "a great image-builder."

▲ As if it really needed more oomph, the LT5 engine in the ZR-1 added 30 bhp (now 405), plus 15 lbs/ft of torque.

▲ Tech tweaks for the ZR-1 included porting/polishing the V-8 heads and a switch to four-bolt main bearings.

▲ The Corvette convertible sold for $42,650 with the 40th anniversary package. Offered also on the coupe, it included an exclusive "ruby red" exterior and interior.

◄ Special chrome emblems went on hood, deck, and side gills of anniversary editions, as did headrest embroidery.

▼ Wheel hubs of the 40th anniversary Corvette were ruby red, color-keyed to the body. Convertibles got a red top.

1993 Selected Colors

Ruby Red Met.	Arctic White
Black	Bright Aqua Met.
Competition Yellow	Torch Red

ENGINE SPECS

1993	LT1	LT5
Type:	ohv V-8	dohc V-8
Bore X stroke (in.):	4.00 X 3.48	3.90 X 3.66
Displacement (ci):	350	350
Compression ratio:	10.5:1	11.0:1
Horsepower @ rpm (bhp):	300 @ 5000	405 @ 5800
Torque @ rpm (lbs/feet):	340 @ 3600	385 @ 5200
Fuel Delivery:	Multi-Port Injection	Multi-Port Injection
Transmission:	4-speed automatic, 6-speed manual	6-speed manual

DIMENSIONS

Wheelbase (in.):	96.2
Overall length (in.):	178.5
Overall height (in.):	46.3
Overall width (in.):	70.7 (73.1 ZR-1)
Track front/rear (in.):	57.7/59.1 (60.6 ZR-1)
Curb weight (lbs):	3333 (3505 ZR-1)

► If a ZR-1 simply wouldn't satisfy, how about a handbuilt Greenwood G572 Corvette? Billed as a "uniquely American response to the supercars from Europe," the $179,333 ultra-coupe measured 76 inches across its stern, to accept 13-inch (19-inch diameter) wheels. Under the hood: a 572-cid (9.4-liter) V-8, blasting out 575 horsepower and a mammoth 700 lbs/ft of torque. With Hydra-Matic, it could shoot to 60 mph in around 3.5 seconds, turn 11.5-second quarter-miles, and hit near 218 mph.

I N D E X